Almost forgotten in the land of her birth-Hawaii, a debt of gratitude to
Pat Masters for this book which brings back to present memory the captivating
life including spiritual journey and contributions of Mary Elizabeth Mikahala
Robinson Foster, one of the greatest benefactors of Buddhism in the world
including Jodo Shinshu in Hawaii.

Rev. Eric Matsumoto,
Bishop,
Honpa Hongwanji Mission of Hawaii

This beautifully written work on philanthropist and social activist Mary Foster,
a Hawaiian noble woman, provides valuable long-lost historical information
on little known aspects of Buddhism's migration to the west as well as its
restoration in its homeland, India

Kathryn Ann Harper, Ph.D.
Professor Emeritus
Loyola Marymount University

In a rare combination, both labor of love and scholarship, Masters gives us an untold story linking spiritual quests across time and space: Hawai`i nei and Sri Lanka, Polynesian and Buddhist streams of spiritual practice, antiquity and modernity. In our fraught historical moment, this book offers illumination, solace and aspiration.

Caroline Sinavaiana Gabbard, Ph.D.
Professor of English (retired)
University of Hawai`i at Manoa

Searching for Mary Foster is an important book that returns to public memory the legacy of a largely forgotten woman who was instrumental in establishing Japanese Buddhism in Hawaii and whose philanthropic generosity impacted the lives of many. In part biography, in part the story of unraveling the mystery that surrounds the life of Mary Foster, the author's own pilgrimage around the world is vividly woven through the book, inviting the reader in on the journey of piecing together this intriguing story via fragments uncovered in temples, archives, even hospitals. This gives the book a freshness and originality that kept me engaged until the last page.

Kerstin Pilz, Phd
writeyourjourney.com

Searching for Mary Foster

Nineteenth-Century Native Hawaiian Buddhist, Philanthropist, and Social Activist

Patricia Lee Masters

Searching for Mary Foster
Nineteenth-Century Native Hawaiian
Buddhist, Philanthropist, and Social Activist

By
Patricia Lee Masters

Copyright © 2017, ABSC, New York

For Patricia Lee Masters

Cover photograph of Mary Foster
courtesy of the Bishop Museum Archives
1525 Bernice Street, Honolulu, HI 96817-2704

Permission to publish this work was arranged with the
Buddhist Study Center, Honpa Hongwanji Mission of Hawaii
1436 University Avenue, Honolulu, HI 96822

Library of Congress Control Number: 2017959473

ISBN # 978-0-9764594-5-3

First edition 2017

Published by
American Buddhist Study Center
331 Riverside drive
New York, NY 10025

Distributed by
Buddhist Study Center
1436 University Avenue
Honolulu, HI 96822

Book designed by Brian Funai

For Amy Agbayani

~ Friend and Mentor ~

CONTENTS

PROLOGUE

One day in October of 1893 an extraordinary meeting took place in Honolulu Harbor on the deck of the *Oceania*. The ship had stopped briefly for refueling on a journey across thousands of miles. A wealthy, aristocratic Hawaiian woman went aboard to meet a slight, young Sinhalese man en route home to Sri Lanka. He was returning from Chicago, after delivering an address on Buddhist philosophy to the first Parliament of World Religions at the World Exposition. Anagarika Dharmapala and Mary Elizabeth Mikahala Robinson Foster were meeting for the first time at the urging of mutual acquaintances, but each experienced an uncanny sense of recognition. Both were lifelong spiritual seekers, and both were indigenous to island countries at a turbulent period in their respective histories. For the remainder of both lives, the ensuing friendship and collaboration was to benefit countless beings.

When I first discovered the story of this unlikely partnership, I was mystified. As a longtime Buddhist scholar, teacher, and resident of Honolulu, how could such a significant chapter in history have escaped my notice? What follows is my exploration of that mystery, of Mary Foster's life. It is a story that was until now all but erased from public memory. How could someone who had such an impact in the world be so unknown, so unacknowledged, especially in her homeland of Hawai`i nei? How is it that she is revered in India and Sri Lanka and yet, few in Honolulu know that Foster Botanical Gardens was not only her home, but the seat of an underground resistance movement in the late 1800s?

How is it that someone who devoted herself to the well-being of her people in a catastrophic period—the overthrow of the Hawaiian kingdom by the United States and its ensuing chaos for the archipelago—be so little-known today? Where was the tale of her foiling the plans of foreign speculators by buying up as much land as she could in Kalama Valley as a refuge for displaced Hawaiians? Of her buying hospital beds at Kapiolani Hospital for those who could not pay? Of sponsoring scholarships for Hawaiian children to the prestigious Kamehameha Schools?

These are the questions that plagued me throughout my research.

Mary Foster's life bridged the nineteenth and twenties centuries, but it traversed more than time. A mixed-blood daughter of Hawai`i, she was a determined visionary, a quiet rebel even in her youth, who broke free of the confinement of a missionary-influenced upbringing. Unusual for her time, she forged a distinguished life for herself by devoting her considerable wealth, efforts, and compassion to alleviate human suffering.

Chapter One

SARNATH, INDIA ~ 1996 ~

The House of Fragrant Truth

It was a sun-filled morning. My motor rickshaw sputtered to a stop in front of a Buddhist temple near a lovely park full of luxuriant trees and small spotted deer grazing here and there. Fellow pilgrims were circumambulating an ancient stone *stupa* (shrine) more than 100 feet high. I was in India teaching in an American Buddhist Studies program based in Bodh Gaya, a small village in northern India well known as the place where the historical Buddha had achieved enlightenment 2500 years ago. In previous semesters I had taken students on weekend excursions to Varanasi, on the banks of the Ganges, visiting many sacred sites in the area, but this was my first visit to Sarnath. The temple had been completed in 1931 to commemorate the site of Buddha's first teachings as an enlightened being (c. 528 BCE). Given the temple's humble appearance, visitors might miss the historical significance of "Mulagandhakuti," (house of fragrant truth): the site where spiritual wisdom was imparted, and words spoken that would reverberate across the world for millennia. But, I had read about Sarnath's deer park and the Mulagandhakuti temple. I was familiar with the Mahabodhi Society that built the temple and worked for decades to perpetuate Buddhist teachings. I had crossed the world from my home in Honolulu, and was thrilled to realize my dream of standing in Sarnath, the genesis of Buddhist teachings.

The temple's outer walls are made of rose-hued stone, easily visible in the surrounding landscape. Marble steps and columned porticos frame the entrance to the main hall. Nearby, vibrantly colored Tibetan and Bhutanese temples make a bright contrast to this modest, subtler neighbor. An inscribed marble plaque in the entranceway reads:

Mulagandhakuti Temple
Erected by
The Anagarika Dharmapala
Founder and General Secretary of
The Mahabodhi Society
With the generous help of
Mrs. Mary Elizabeth Foster
Of Honolulu, and others
On the site where
Lord Buddha
Promulgated the teachings 2,500 years ago

Mary Elizabeth Foster? Of Honolulu? I had lived in Honolulu for over forty years. I am a Buddhist, and I had studied and taught Buddhism for many years. I knew the name Foster from somewhere, but could not immediately place it. All I could think of was the Foster Botanical Gardens, a green sanctuary in downtown Honolulu. It was a place where I had spent a good deal of time—meditating, reflecting, walking among the trees. In fact, a Bodhi tree from Sri Lanka, propagated from the tree in India where Buddha achieved enlightenment, grows in that garden. Other than a sign noting that Mary Foster had lived there, I knew nothing else about the garden's namesake. Intrigued, I wondered if there might be any relationship between the two.

In the temple's main hall, I passed exquisite paintings that depicted the paradigmatic turns of the Buddha's life, subtle masterpieces by the Japanese artist Kosetsu Nosu, whose calling it was to paint the scenes in the temple. Encouraged by Rabindranath Tagore, the great Indian humanist and Nobel Prize–winning writer, Kosetsu spent five years (1932–1936), painting the murals. The inner sanctum held a young monk attending to the altar. Startled by my Sri Lankan greeting, "Ayubowan," he turned. I explained that I was from Honolulu, but was unfamiliar with the Mary Foster from the plaque. He said, "Madam, you must be knowing her. She was a wonderful person to whom we Buddhists owe a great deal."

The monk took me into his office behind the main statue of the Buddha on the central altar, and began to talk. His eyes were alight with the excitement telling what he knew of Mary Foster. Part Hawaiian, she had been born in Honolulu. In 1893 she had met the great Buddhist teacher Anagarika Dharmapala as he passed through Honolulu on his way home to Sri Lanka (then known as Ceylon). He was returning from the first Parliament of World Religions in Chicago where he had been one of the keynote speakers. His ship, the *Oceania*, was stopping in Honolulu for one day and he had arranged to meet Mary Foster on the advice of some acquaintances in Chicago. He was told that she would support his work to alleviate the suffering of others. He was told that she was open-minded, a spiritual seeker who would be sympathetic to his teachings.

Some of the story was already familiar to me. I had heard about Dharmapala in Chicago, while attending the centennial anniversary of the first Parliament of World Religions in 1993. One hundred years earlier Dharmapala and the great Hindu master Vivekananda had captivated attendees with their eloquent introduction to the religious beliefs of the East. Now, I was struck by the historical confluence of these events: Dharmapala's trip home, his meeting with Mary Foster, and the political disturbances destabilizing the Hawaiian nation. It was in that very year, 1893, that the machinations of American businessmen and missionary descendants finally led to the overthrow of the Hawaiian monarchy, the imposition of martial law and the house arrest of the Hawaiian Queen, Lili'uokalani.

The monk's tale inspired a flurry of questions. I had already spent many years traveling to Sri Lanka and was aware of Anagarika Dharmapala's importance to his country and people. What drew him to Mary Foster, and what took place during their momentous meeting aboard a ship in Honolulu harbor, an encounter that was to change both of their lives? Why did I suddenly feel an uncanny connection to this story? I too had been drawn to the wisdom of Buddhism and spent years traveling, studying in academic settings, and practicing. What had drawn me to settle in Hawai`i were its many cultures, traditions, and practices of Buddhism. Suddenly, it felt as though I were meant to know more about this Mary Foster and her singular life. After visiting with the monk,

I slowly returned to exploring Sarnath's sacred monuments, but now thinking about Mary Foster and wondering.

Chapter Two

HONOLULU

Back in Hawai`i, I began my investigation on the edge of town at Foster Gardens. If anything, friends and acquaintances knew little more than I did about the woman who had once lived there. Paul Weissich, former director of the Gardens from 1957 through 1989, remembered beginning his tenure and seeing staff throwing out boxes stored in rooms destined to become their new offices. "I often wondered if any of those boxes might have contained precious items and papers that belonged to Mary Foster," he confessed. Sharing many stories he had heard from people who knew her personally, Weissich recommended that I explore the Hawai'i State Archives. Apparently, "many of Mary Foster's papers had been turned over to the Hawaiian Trust Company and eventually to the Hawai'i State Archives around 1968."

At the Archives I was surprised to find dozens of boxes containing Mary Foster's financial records, business correspondence, land and property papers. The most intriguing box contained a folder of her personal papers. Opening that folder was like discovering hidden treasure. The papers were loose and disordered, as if other hands had shuffled them in earlier searches. Her full name was Mary Elizabeth Mikahala Robinson. Born on September 21, 1844, she was the first-born of Rebecca Kaikilani Prever, a native of Maui, and James Robinson, a British shipbuilder.

I found a death certificate, indicating that she had passed away on December 19, 1930 "at home." The address on the certificate turned out to be that of Victoria Ward, her younger sister. Apparently, Foster spent the last five months of her life at the Ward estate, known as the "Old Plantation." In the preceding years, she had traveled back and forth to San Francisco, staying either in a home she owned there, at the elegant Clift Hotel, or with friends. Her will contained codicils modifying the original documents and witnessed by two of her friends in San Francisco the year before she died. Surprisingly, the signers were neither not family members nor close friends of the family. The meaning of this would become clear much later.

One letter in the personal folder was especially captivating. It was from Countess Constance Wachtmeister of New York, dated July 29, 1894, inviting Mary Foster to join her in traveling to India at the end of that year. Countess Wachtmeister was a close friend of Madame Blavatsky, founder of the Theosophical Society, living with her for many years and looking after Blavatsky's personal papers. I began to wonder about Foster's other friends and associates on the continent and abroad. What, if any, was her relationship with the Theosophical Society, one of the most influential philosophical movements of her time? Did Foster accept the countess's invitation to travel? If so, did they go to Bodh Gaya or to Sarnath? Did they join Dharmapala or any of the Theosophists there? Did she ever make to India at all?

Outside the archives, the sky had clouded over. Aside from a smattering of notes, letter fragments and financial documents, the folder seemed to provide more questions than answers. For a privileged, well-traveled Hawaiian woman from a highly literate culture, it seemed odd to find so little written evidence of such a singular, exciting life in her personal papers. Had documents been lost? If they were not in the Archives, where were they? A few days later, the State Archivist uncovered a genealogical study of the Robinson family. This would help me to better understand Foster's family and their influence on her life.

Robinson Family Background
Rebecca Kaikilani Prever

Mary Foster's mother, Rebecca Prever, was born on January 7, 1817, at Waihale, Honokowai, Ka'anapali on the island of Maui. She was half Native Hawaiian and half French. Descended from chiefly lines in Maui and Hawai'i island (Hilo and Ka'u), she was called Kaikilani by relatives. Others called her Rebecca. Like other chiefs at that time, hers had been displaced from their ancestral lands during the years that Kamehameha had been fighting to unite the islands. In his book about Foster's sister, Victoria Ward, their grandnephew Frank Hustace Jr. wrote:

"It was an unstable period and many families were swept up in the confusion of shifting loyalties, uncertainty and change. Foreign visitors were arriving with increased frequency, and their customs and morality were beginning to undermine the age-old social structure of the Hawaiian people." [1]

In those days, haoles (foreigners) filled the streets of Lahaina, Maui, and the islands were in turmoil. The Prever family history illustrates the kind of far-reaching social change underway at the time. Rebecca Prever was the firstborn of one of the earliest marriages between a Native Hawaiian woman and a haole man. At first resisting inter-marriage, Hawaiians gradually realized its inevitability as well as its potential to help negotiate the turbulent social environment, especially after the decimation of their people from foreign diseases. The haole who married into Native families were often won over to the Hawaiians' cause, transformed by their generosity and kindness, becoming fiercely protective of Hawaiians in business transactions and other negotiations with foreigners. Some of them would prove to be instrumental in the rebellions that arose to resist the illegal takeover of the Islands in 1893.

Rebecca Prever's family was no exception. Her father, Jean Adam Previere, had come from France around 1790, perhaps a sailor who jumped ship in Lahaina, took a liking to the Islands and decided to stay. He anglicized his name to John Prever and quickly became part of the Lahaina community, operating a thriving business as a broker negotiating agreements between foreign sea captains and Native Hawaiians regarding provisions, services, and trade. According to the nineteenth-century historian Abraham Fornander, it had become common for "every chief of note to have one or more foreigners in his employ. They were serviceable as interpreters and factors in trading with the foreign ships; and their skill and adroitness in handling firearms, and in many other things hitherto unknown to the Hawaiians, made them valuable to the chiefs." [2] Working closely with the chiefs, the aliʻi (the aristocrats), and foreign businessmen, he soon became involved in Hawaiian affairs and married the beautiful Kamakana (gift of all gifts).³

Gift of all Gifts
Kamakana
Rebecca's mother Kamakana was born in Kohala on Hawai'i Island to Maunahina and Napu'upahoehoe. Shortly after her birth, Kamakana was adopted by the Kohala chief, Keaweaweulaokalani. Legend tells of the chief who, growing tired of all of the warring on Hawai'i Island, moved his family to Maui. A story of their perilous crossing of the Ahanuinui Channel, the longest and most difficult passage between the Islands, relates how they were saved by a family of great white sharks, and how the shark became the protector ('aumakua) of the family. Once on Maui, the chief and his family lived a more peaceful life, blessed by their new home in a fertile valley with abundant water and ready access to rich farm land and the bountiful ocean. The young Kamakana thrived in their home at the mouth of Honokowai stream near an inland fishpond, swimming and playing in the valley with her hanai (adopted) brothers.

In her early teens, Kamakana met and married John Prever and eventually moved to Waihale with their nine children. It was a time of sprawling growth and activity in Lahaina, with ships of many nations visiting and merchants opening businesses to fill the needs of the ever-increasing visitors. John Prever, a successful and trusted trader, served many of them. His children were schooled at home by their mother who taught them to live with love, harmony, and gratitude for the beauty and great blessings of their land. Kaikilani Rebecca Prever, Mary Foster's mother, was their eldest child. She was described as a loving child, the favorite of her father. Hustace wrote of her childhood as quiet and filled with familial love.³ When Kaikilani met and married John James Robinson in 1843, her life was to change dramatically.

James Robinson
John James Robinson, a successful British shipbuilder, frequently traveled to Maui from O'ahu on business. He had many friends and acquaintances in Maui

who would have known the Prever family and could likely have introduced them. Robinson was a widower with two children, James and Charlotte, whose first wife had died in early 1843. Later that year he requested Rebecca Prever's hand in marriage in a letter to her father. John Prever answered making Rebecca's agreement a condition for his consent. Prever's open-mindedness, unusual for the time, was a precursor to the adventurous nature of his future child, Mary.

To Mr. James Robinson
At the Point
Honolulu, Oahu
Lahaina, October 26, 1843

Dear Sir:
In answer to your letter of October 21st, I have to say that you have my full consent and also my daughter Rebecca's consent and shall be happy to see you whenever it is convenient to you.

Please give myself and my family's respects to Mr. Thompson and his family and accept the same from yours truly, John A. Prever [5]

The couple was married in a service that was performed by the American missionary, their friend Asa Thurston, on December 22 in Kailua. Soon after, the couple settled in Honolulu. James Robinson was an enterprising young man, and John Prever found him a great addition to the family. Robinson's parents, Durham and Mary Summer Robinson, welcomed Rebecca Prever into their family from England.

James Robinson had been born on December 9, 1798, in London. It was a time of empire building and industrialization in Great Britain. Having recently lost their thirteen American colonies, the British had rebounded as explorers; their trade ships were traveling the oceans seeking wealth in new places. Cook's travels and reports from the Pacific in the 1770s opened the region to burgeoning trade. Hawai'i's central location between East and West, and plentiful produce, fruit, fish, and fresh water made it a port of call for many ships originating in Britain.

Many young Englishmen from all social classes were intrigued by reports of newly "discovered" lands. James Robinson was among those who had dreamed of exotic places and adventures on the high seas. He grew up loving the sea, and in 1820 at the age of twenty-two, he sailed to Hawai'i as a carpenter's apprentice on the whaling ship *Hermes*. At Cape Horn the *Hermes* passed the American ship *Thaddeus,* which was carrying the first company of New England missionaries to Hawai'i. *Hermes* preceded *Thaddeus'* arrival in Honolulu Harbor by two weeks. James Robinson was later fond of saying that he had beaten the missionaries to the Islands. He returned to London, but two years later Robinson was back in Hawai'i.

In October of 1822, after an eventful voyage, challenged by shipwreck and a recycled schooner—aptly named *Deliverance*—Robinson had arrived in Honolulu with a small crew. There they found a quiet village with thatched hale (houses) on a fertile plain surrounded by valleys and a shoreline offering deep harbors. Although the hale predominated, there were some Western buildings, including a warehouse built for Kamehameha to store goods bought from trade ships arriving from Asia, Europe, and America. The surrounding ocean and reef provided an abundance of fish and other seafood, augmented by Hawaiian fishponds created to stock a year-round supply. For millennia the Hawaiians had been wise stewards of their islands, recognizing and honoring their interdependence with the natural world. Because of its many and varied resources, Honolulu was soon to become a busy port. With the diminishing number of whales off Lahaina, Honolulu became a newfound destination for many in the growing Pacific trade.

The talented, enterprising Robinson quickly found his niche among both ali'i and the foreigners in Honolulu. He became friends with the Regent Ka'ahumanu and the young king, with whom he enjoyed an affectionate relationship for the remainder of their lives. Robinson and his childhood friend Robert George

Lawrence remained in Honolulu, eventually selling the schooner *Deliverance*—which they had salvaged from the wreckage of their original ship en route to Hawai`i. The proceeds of $2000 from the sale was to finance the establishment of their shipbuilding business. Partners Lawrence and Robinson found land for their business near the residence of the king and his regent, Ka‘ahumanu.

Kamehameha II

Kamehameha II was ruling the Islands when the *Deliverance* arrived in Honolulu. Kamehameha I's oldest royal offspring, Liholiho ‘Iolani, came to the throne at twenty-three after his father's death in 1819. Officially named Kamehameha II, he preferred to be called ‘Iolani, though most of those close to him called him Liholiho. Politically naïve, he was caught between the Hawaiian traditions of his youth and the new realities brought to the Islands by foreigners. Ka‘ahumanu, his father's favorite wife, was made Kuhina Nui, or Regent, to the young prince. She claimed that the king had bestowed the title upon her on his deathbed. It was she who actually ruled, while Liholiho performed the ceremonial duties of the throne. Liholiho's own mother, Keopuolani, was in poor health and could not assume the Kuhina Nui role, but she worked closely with Ka‘ahumanu in ruling the kingdom.[6] In fact, it was the two queen-regents who pushed for and oversaw the collapse of the old order.

The initial signal of significant social change occurred at a feast given by Liholiho soon after his father's death. The two queen-regents broke the ancient kapu (taboo) against men and women eating together, when they sat down with Liholiho's younger brother Kauikeaouli to share food. Then, at a chiefly feast in Kailua-Kona in November of 1819, the new king sat at the women's table and began to eat his meal. With that, there was a cry of "Ai noa, the eating kapu is broken."[7]

Many say that Ka‘ahumanu and Keopuolani influenced Liholiho to take such bold steps. Others have claimed that it was Liholiho's own interest in Christianity and the ways of the haole in Hawai‘i that caused him to condemn traditional cultural practices. Hawaiian women have always wielded significant cultural authority, so it is not surprising that Ka‘ahumanu and Keopuolani could have brought about such momentous change. Liholiho was also an impulsive man, and his youthful penchant for novelty could have come into play. Whatever the cause, traditions were being challenged and changed during that period. In 1824 Liholiho died of measles at twenty-eight while visiting Britain. His son, Kamehameha III (Kauikeaouli) was only twelve years old at the time, so Ka`ahumanu continued as Kuhina Nui, shepherding the young monarch as she had done with his father. She ruled the Islands as Regent until her death in 1832.

Pākākā

In 1827, Robinson and Lawrence obtained land for their shipbuilding business from Kalanimoku, King Kamehameha's chief advisor and the prime minister of Hawai'i. The site of a sixteenth century heiau (temple), destroyed by missionaries several years earlier, Pākākā was located at the eastern end of Honolulu Harbor.[8]

The ancient temple was well known to Hawaiians as a place of mystery, a site where the high priests of O'ahu adorned the walls with the heads of men offered in sacrifice. Opposite the heiau was a large boulder with thumb-sized holes where the chiefs would gather to play kōnane, a game like Chinese checkers. Stories are still told about people gambling away their land and even their lives at the site.

When James Robinson arrived at Pākākā, Liholiho and Ka'ahumanu were living in a large hale (house) adjacent to the fort. Learning of the site's history, Robinson became concerned about building on desecrated ground. So, he consulted a Hawaiian priest (kahuna) about blessing the land before disturbing it with construction. Robinson's tact about the sensitive matter endeared him to Hawaiians, who came to call him Kimo Pākākā. James and Bobby built the first shipyard in Hawai'i at Pākākā, James Robinson & Company, Shipbuilders. They remained partners of the successful business until James's death in 1876. According to the family, theirs may have been the first business partnership in Hawai'i. Bobby Lawrence and the firm remained at Pākākā until 1925, when the site was condemned and replaced by what is now Pier 11, near the Aloha Tower.

Because of its distinctive step-gabled roof, the Pākākā building became a land-mark which appeared in many photographs and paintings of the period. Easily recognized with its two stories of coral rock walls and top floor loft, the building contained office space, living quarters, warehouse, and cafeteria for workers. In 1869, the Robinsons gave a grand ball on the second floor, in honor of the Duke of Edinburgh who was visiting the Islands.

Both Robinson and Lawrence were astute businessmen, adaptable to change, modifying their business as times required. When the sailing ships and whales declined in number, they diversified and began to import lumber from the Pacific Northwest to accommodate the growing influx of foreigners wanting Western-style buildings. Robinson began the first interisland shipping company, and built shipping vessels as well as sailing ships, and schooners for pleasure travel around the Islands. Soon, however, Hawai'i was being overwhelmed by problems from the growing number of speculators and land developers flocking to the islands.

The Mahele

The Mahele was a hierarchical land distribution system established in the 1850s, thanks to the collusion of missionary and business interests. It was tantamount to institutionalized burglary. It was a body blow to an ancient culture, a society that had stewarded their `āina (land) with exquisite skill for millennia. For the first time in history Hawaiian land was commodified and sold; for the first time it could be "owned." It could "belong" to individuals. What was sacred was profaned. From antiquity land had been communally held by Hawaiians, their organizational philosophy a collective, interdependent one. Now, land became objectified; it was reduced to "property" that could be bought and sold to the highest bidder. The Mahele inflicted catastrophic damage on the Hawaiian people; it took not only their land, but their self-determination, their political power. James Robinson (and later his daughter Mary) joined in the struggle to protect Hawaiian lands, to protect the `āina being devoured by investors and speculators swarming to the Islands. They helped Hawaiians negotiate the new rules, to protect themselves and their lands from the blight of new regulations set forth in a foreign language.

Amid those tumultuous times, James and Rebecca started their family. They had nine children, most of them were to live long, successful lives. Mary Elizabeth Mikahala was the eldest of nine: six daughters and three sons. Her siblings were to make significant contributions to her life.[10] Hawaiian was the first language in the household, but Robinson insisted that his children master English as well. The family honored their Hawaiian traditions and cultural practices. Loyalty to their heritage was extremely important to several of the children, most of all to Mary.

Mary Elizabeth Mikahala

Mary was the only child of Rebecca and James who was not born in the Old Homestead, which James would later build in Nuʻuanu for the family. Before the Old Homestead was completed, they lived at Pākākā. When the second child Victoria was born, Mary was two, and the family moved into their new home. The Old Homestead was elegant, made of rose white coral and stone, perched on a hill in one of the most beautiful parts of Honolulu. With the Koʻolau mountain range rising behind it, the house had an ocean view and was cooled by Nuʻuanu breezes. It stood on two and a half acres, just mauka (toward the mountains) of the newly built Oʻahu Cemetery on what is now Robinson Lane. In her serialized "Tales about Hawaii," Clarice Taylor writes:

The house was very modern for that day. It had kerosene lamps; was built of coral blocks cut out of the reef and had a lanai all around…Beautiful trees and banks of roses blossomed in the yard. A horse and buggy could be driven to about where the Kawananakoa Middle School stands today and then travelers and visitors went afoot or rode horseback up the hill to the Robinson home. The house stood until 1908 and was home to four generations of the Robinson family.[11]

Like other wealthy kamaʻaina families (those born in Hawaiʻi or longtime residents), the Robinsons were becoming increasingly successful in both politics and business. Many of the most successful businesses and charitable institutions throughout the Islands grew from the work of the illustrious Robinson family.

The Oʻahu Charity School

The children attended private schools including the Catholic School on Fort Street, Kamehameha Schools, and Punahou. The Royal School, set up by King Kamehameha III in 1839, was limited to the children of the Royal family and aliʻi. Mission schools had been established to "educate the 'heathens' to become good Christian citizens."[12]

In the mission schools, Hawaiian children were educated solely in the Hawaiian language and curriculum, which limited their opportunities for success in the increasingly pluralistic society. After translating the Bible into Hawaiian, missionaries used it to teach reading. All subjects were taught through Biblical perspectives. By controlling subject matter and limiting study to the Hawaiian language, missionaries were ensuring their domination of the native population. Attempting to raise "good natives," the missionaries manipulated Hawaiians, thereby restricting their awareness of and ability to communicate with the outside world.[13] Around 1832 Honolulu merchants and seamen began to plan their own school; many of them had married Native women and wanted their children to be educated in English. They felt that their children were discriminated against at the Mission schools and wanted the children to be have a proper education.

The maritime and merchant communities quickly raised money to build their school, and the king granted an allotment of land with the condition that native tenants be compensated for relocating. The community chose seven trustees to manage construction and establishment of the school. James Robinson was among the first trustees, playing an active role in the school's creation and continued success. The Charity School officially opened in January 1833 with thirty-five students, both boys and girls, taught by Andrew Johnstone and his wife. It was located on the Waikīkī side of the present Judiciary building on Mililani Lane. The lane ran from King Street to Queen Street, adjacent to the site of the future Kawaiahaʻo Church.

The school became a refuge for mixed race children, some of whom had been orphaned by disease or the loss of their fathers at sea. It was a haven for those with parents frequently away on long voyages, and children were often housed with the Johnstones' or other families in the school community. The curriculum was developed by the parents and the Johnstones. It included Hawaiian history and language along with other rigorous courses, such as mathematics and literature, modeled after those taught in academies in Britain and the continent. Soon after the school opened, the Johnstones were recalled to Boston by their sponsors, the ABCFM (American Board of Commissions of Foreign Missions). Chastised for teaching in English rather than in Hawaiian, and for challenging the Mission schools' teaching methods, the Johnstones resigned from the Mission to stay with the Charity School until 1844 when they opened their own school.[14]

The Robinson children were friends with many other part-Hawaiian children whose parents were in the mercantile and shipping businesses. Many of the families lived in the Nu'uanu area, some worshipping with the Robinsons at St. Andrew's Cathedral, established in the Islands in 1862. The Robinsons and the Hawaiian royals were also very close, partly because of Mary's mother, Rebecca's ali'i lineage, and also because of James Robinson's close friendship with John Young, the grandfather of Queen Emma. Mary Foster and Lydia Paki, the future Queen Lili'uokalani, were about the same age and close friends. Queen Emma was fond of inviting the children to her home for dinners and picnics, and Mary and Lydia spent happy times together there.

From a young age, both Lili'uokalani and Mary Foster were curious about different spiritual beliefs and religions. In a letter from 1894, Mary Foster wrote about her early experiences at school and her need to know more about spiritual ideas other than Christianity, including her own native traditions and practices. "My hunger for understanding remains unquenched," she wrote, "and I long for some way to better understand the world, God, and myself."[15] As an adult she invited the queen to attend services at a Buddhist temple; the queen wrote about it in her own diary as a "profound spiritual experience."[16] Mary Foster continued her spiritual search throughout her life, finally settling on a Buddhist path. This choice was to have a profound impact on her thinking and actions in later life.

As a young woman, Foster was adventurous and curious with expanding interests in many different areas. At sixteen, she married Thomas Foster on April 4, 1861. Nine years her senior, he had come to Hawai'i five years earlier from Nova Scotia. Soon after arriving, he went to work for Mary's father. He was hard-working, and James Robinson had taken an immediate liking to him.

Thomas Foster

A native Canadian, Thomas Foster had been born in Nova Scotia in 1835. He and his brother had worked in shipbuilding since their youth and, in 1855 decided to try working in the business in Hawai'i.[17] While still working for Robinson, Thomas began to build what would later become the Inter-Island Steam Navigation Company. His first fleet of steamers was built in Port Ludlow, Washington. In the 1880s, he initiated the first inter-island mail delivery service in Hawai'i. Soon, the Company expanded beyond mail delivery to include varieties of cargo such as livestock, home furnishings and food items.

Thomas also built schooners, the first in 1876, naming it the *Mikahala* for his wife; and a second, in 1879, the *James Makee* for his Scottish friend, former sea captain and owner of the Rose Ranch on Maui. Another of his ships was called *C.R. Bishop* after a man he greatly admired, Charles Reed Bishop.[18] Mary Foster and Bernice Pauahi Bishop, Charles's wife, were good friends. The four-some spent time together at the Bishops' home, Haleakala, where Mrs. Bishop had a lovely garden that she managed herself. Foster admired Mrs. Bishop whose good works inspired her. They worked together on several social service projects. When Mrs. Bishop created the Kamehameha Schools, Mary Foster endowed several scholarships, most of them for girls.[19]

Mary and Thomas were able to buy their first home, with help from Mary's father, just above the property that later became Foster Garden in Honolulu. In 1884 they built their home with a five-story tower, a "widow's walk" which allowed Thomas to see his ships and watch over business in the ports. The family legend is that after Thomas died, Foster lit a candle in the tower every evening in honor of her deceased husband. I recently learned from David Forbes, a distinguished researcher of that period, that the candle sat on a Buddhist altar that she lit every evening.

The interior of her home would probably have been much like that of her sister Victoria's, seen in family photos—Persian rugs, inlaid china cabinets and horsehair rockers. There would have been Hawaiian furnishings and precious objects such as feather lei, kahili (feather standard, symbol of royalty) and kapa (mulberry bark cloth) coverlets as well. Mary's library would likely have contained such books as Edwin Arnold's *Light of Asia*, Blavatsky's *Isis Unveiled*, Henry Steel Olcott's *Buddhist Catechism*, Whitman's *Leaves of Grass*, Buddhaghosa's *The Path of Purification*, Thoreau's *Walden*, and the essays of Ralph Waldo Emerson. Her intellectual curiosity would lead her to organize a private salon in her home for spiritual thinkers and leaders, whom she had invited to the Islands, to gather for conversation and fellowship. Her salon became a refuge for those seeking knowledge of spiritual traditions other than the Christianity that dominated the Islands. It may also have been a meeting place for those who worked to re-establish the monarchy after the overthrow of Queen Lili'uokalani.

The gardens of the Foster Estate were filled with lush vegetation. Certainly, Mary enjoyed the gardens during her life with Thomas, and she spent much of her time adding to the collection of botanicals from the original estate. She later enlisted the help of the botanist Harold Lyon, who had come to Honolulu to work for the Hawai'i Sugar Planters Association. Hired by the planters to research diseases related to sugar plantations, he and Mary Foster created one of the most beautiful botanical gardens in America.

Mary and Thomas were unable to have children, but they shared happiness, great comfort and social standing. Together, they sought to understand the changing times and their place in Hawai'i. They shared compassionate natures and business acumen. Their investments throughout the state and on the west coast thrived under their joint management. For a time, it seemed as if nothing could fail them. Then, in 1889 Thomas suddenly took ill while they were visiting San Francisco, staying at the Occidental Hotel. He became increasingly weak and subsequently died at fifty-four. For some years, it was exceedingly difficult for Mary to recover from the loss, and she spent much of her time traveling, far from her home and family. When in Honolulu, she mostly stayed at her sister Victoria's home, and the Foster Estate fell into disrepair. Apparently, she could not bear to live in her home any longer. When she visited the estate, overgrown and neglected, she felt great loneliness and sadness. She finally decided to leave it as it was for a time. It became a kīpuka, an abandoned oasis in the middle of the city.

After an extended period of grief, Mary finally began to take the steps that would set her life on a dramatically different course. She was forty-eight years old. Her political, philanthropic, and spiritual interests multiplied, and her life was increasingly filled with diverse people with wide-ranging ideas. It is likely that her family found her eclectic interests and acquaintances bohemian. Such pursuits may have alienated Mary from some relatives who questioned her judgment and taste in things unfamiliar to them. Nonetheless, she continued seeking out like-minded friends, both in Honolulu and abroad, as she sought a spiritual path that could quench her longing for inner peace.

Chapter Three

COLOMBO, CEYLON

Ceylon

The name conjures visions of an island paradise, much like Mary Foster's Hawai'i. It had been variously named The Mango Island, The Tear Drop Island, and the Pearl Earring of India. In ancient times, Greek geographers called it Taprobane and Arabs referred to it as Serendib, the origin of the word serendipity. Ceilão was the name given by the Portuguese when they arrived on the island in 1505, and it was later transliterated into English as Ceylon. Some say that the word ceilão was a derivative of "heavenly." All of the names connote a magical place, a place of serenity and peace.

The small tropical island at the southeast tip of India was anything but peaceful when Anagarika Dharmapala was born. The year was 1864 and the British had already established their colonial presence; they were preceded by the Portuguese and the Dutch, bringing not only the mission of Christianity but also the mining of natural resources and the enslavement of Sri Lankans. It was a place of great distress and upheaval. When I arrived on the island in September of 1999, the country was in a similar state of political unrest and civil strife. I had been awarded a Fulbright Fellowship to Sri Lanka to conduct research on Anagarika Dharmapala. Only later would I discover his role as Mary Foster's lifelong friend, confidante, and teacher.

The name Ceylon had been changed to Sri Lanka in 1972, but there remained age-old struggles and rivalries that accompanied that renaming. The players were somewhat different than those in 1864, Dharmapala's birth year, but the issues were similar. In that year Buddhism had been suppressed by Christian missionaries. In 1999, the struggle concerned partly religious rivalries between the Hindu Tamils and the Sinhalese Buddhists. In 1864 British colonial powers decreed that every child born on the island must be given a Christian name. Christian schooling was mandatory for all children. Those who converted to Christianity had more benefits than those who remained Buddhist. The converts were supported with higher education and jobs with the government or Christian companies that dominated the island. Buddhists, particularly in the rural villages, were denied access to higher education and relegated to service jobs in the cities, or to remaining in villages bereft of possibilities for a more prosperous life.

The British were successful in converting mostly Tamils to Christianity. Tamils had been living in Sri Lanka for hundreds of years, continuously arriving from South India. In the eighteenth century, a new, large contingency of Tamil laborers were brought from South India by the British to work on the tea estates that they were establishing in the hills of Ceylon. The Tamils were traditionally Hindu but many of them converted to Christianity once they settled in Sri Lanka. They benefitted from the British schooling that many of them received from the missionaries. Some of the brightest were sent to Britain for higher education and returned as lawyers and doctors. They became wealthy and influential in the country, exacerbating tensions with the Sinhalese Buddhists.

There were protests by Buddhists against the British at that time and an attempted civil war, but it was quickly stopped by the foreigners' guns and the laws they imposed. After the British finally left Ceylon in 1948, tensions continued between the Sinhalese and the Tamils; what began as street brawls escalated into terrorist warfare. A civil war broke out in 1983 over the long held held discrimination against the Sinhalese. The turbulence remained in full force when I arrived in 1999.

I arrived in early September and through the Fulbright Office, was introduced to one of the most illustrious families in the capital city Colombo. The family was Tamil, and it was the first time I had encountered that cultural group in such an intimate way. The Kadirgamar family, with whom I lived, were elite members of Tamil society; educated in London, they had converted to Christianity many years earlier. The brother of the family, Lakshman Kadirgamar, was the foreign minister of the country. A few years after I lived in their home, he was assassinated by an LTTE (Tamil Tiger) sniper.

During the civil war, I lived for more than a year in the Kadirgamar's grand house on Queens Road while researching the details of Anagarika Dharmapala's life. The house was two blocks from the National Archives, and each day I walked to that old stone building and sat on the floor of a private room, surrounded by dusty cardboard boxes filled with Dharmapala's diaries. Those diaries, written in old bound notebooks in Dharmapala's beautiful hand, revealed much about the man, his fascinating recollections and the stories of his life. They were written in English, a result of Dharmapala's schooling under British rule, and many of them contained stories about Mary Foster.

Life before Anagarika

Anagarika Dharmapala was not always known by his title and chosen name. *Anagarika* means "Homeless Seeker" and is a self-chosen title taken without ceremony except for the donning of the white robes that identify one as an Anagarika. Unlike Buddhist monks or nuns who undergo a period of training as novices before being fully ordained, an Anagarika proclaims his intention to leave home and begin a spiritual journey on his own, without the formal guidance of a priest or the company of Buddhist *sangha* (community of the ordained).

Dharmapala, his second chosen name, means "Protector of the Dharma" a moniker he selected in his early twenties when he began his spiritual search in earnest. His birth name was Don David Hewavitarne, and he was born into a wealthy Sinhalese Buddhist family. They were highly respected *goigama* (gentry farmer class) from Matara in the south of the island. Don David's grandfather, Dingiri Appuhamy Hewavitarne had two sons, one of whom became a Buddhist monk named Hittatiya Atthadassi and the other, Don Carolis, Don David's father, a fine furniture maker. Before David was born, Don Carolis moved to Colombo, the fast-growing commercial port city in the 1800s where fine furniture could be easily shipped to countries outside of Ceylon, and where opportunities were abundant. He soon met and married Mallika, the daughter of Andris Perera Dharmagunawardene, a prominent Colombo businessman. Together they opened a furniture manufacturing business in the Pettah area. The couple longed for a child, and when Mallika became pregnant, there were many signs presaging a special birth. Mallika, a very devout Buddhist, felt moved to sleep before a statue of the Buddha in their home each night and during the day, she offered flowers and coconut oil lamps as a blessing and request for a healthy child. Undoubtedly, a woman of her status and position, like others of her time, hoped for a son who would be able to revive Buddhism to its former status as the State religion, after several hundred years of religious suppression.

On the full moon of three successive months before the birth, Buddhist monks were invited to the house to chant from Pali texts and to bless the mother and her unborn baby. On September 17, 1864, Mallika's birthday, Don David was born amid thunder and lightning, an omen in Sri Lanka that signals a powerful birth and perhaps foretells a powerful life.

During my Fulbright fellowship period, people were curious and excited about my research on Anagarika Dharmapala. Dharmapala was and still is highly revered person in Sri Lanka, and the Sinhalese people credit him with bringing Buddhism back to life there. He is regarded as a national hero, and is also viewed as a defender of civil rights and freedom. Sinhalese know the debt that all Buddhists owe him for persevering in his quest to bring the Mahabodhi Temple in Bodh Gaya, India (Buddhism's holiest site), back into the hands of Buddhists. He did not live to see his dream of restoration fully realized. However, in 1949 by order of Prime Minister Nehru, the Mahabodhi did become a Buddhist temple again. With the formal transfer of power occurring in 1951, a management system was developed wherein Buddhists and Hindus worked together to keep the temple safe. Dharmapala had worked tirelessly throughout his life to fulfill that dream.

As a researcher, I wondered why the young man was so dedicated to his quest. Looking into his early years was quite revealing. I found a small book in Colombo called *Flame in Darkness* by the Buddhist monk Sangharakshita that chronicled Dharmapala's life. Dharmapala's early schooling was at the Pettah Catholic School, later known as St. Mary's College. After two years, he felt that the Catholic religion's dislike of his Buddhist tradition was not helpful for his young mind. His parents then enrolled him in a Sinhalese private school where he remained for two years. There he received a strict introduction to Sinhala literature, Buddhist texts and commentaries, but not much more. Dharmapala was intellectually curious and feisty, a young man who questioned authority and thus attracted tensions from the faculties in all of the schools he attended. Eventually, he left the Sinhala school for St. Benedict's College, until he was asked to leave after two years. The following two years were spent at an Anglican boarding school, which afforded him time and opportunity to study Christianity more deeply. He had witnessed the boarding master, who was fond of drinking hard liquor, take delight in shooting small birds that alighted on the branches outside his room. That saddened Dharmapala and, when he spoke to the master about it, the man angrily beat the young Dharmapala. Beatings were not uncommon in the school, and Dharmapala experienced the sting of the cane more than most students. He persisted in his stubborn questioning, and wrote about it in a short piece called "Reminiscences of My Early Life."[1] He recalled an incident where he was sitting quietly, reading a book on the Buddhist Four Noble Truths when the same master approached and demanded the book, tore it up and flung it out the window. Dharmapala became confused and asked what had caused offense; the master told him that there was only one truth. When Dharmapala suggested that there was no conflict between Christian and Buddhist ideas, he was severely beaten again. He became more and more distressed as his education continued.

Another significant incident revealed how his own consciousness had been formed. The incident concerned the death of a fellow student at the school. One of the teachers had invited the students to gather around the dead body and to join in the prayers being offered. As Dharmapala looked at the uneasy faces of his classmates staring at the corpse of their friend, he saw great fear, which was not dispelled but fed by the prayers. He had a flash of illumination that he wrote about in his diary: "prayer that is born of fear helps no one."[2] That experience gave him a sense of freedom from fear that would become one of his most striking qualities; it also provided a different relationship to prayer. "Prayer," he wrote, "should not be used to create or quell fear but to show gratitude and give thanks." He even felt that the traditional use of prayer to ask for personal favor or protection was not an appropriate use. He spoke often about this point.[3]

It is interesting that Dharmapala loved to read the Bible, which he wrote about extensively in his diaries. He found its text strikingly beautiful. He loved the rhythmic diction and the cadences of the poetry. However, he did not read the Bible uncritically and began to formulate questions to ask his teachers. Some of the answers satisfied his young intellect, but others left him perplexed. When he finally left the school, it was because of the poor quality of food rather than the rhetoric. His father had visited one day and found him so emaciated that he pulled him out of the school immediately.

After two months of recovering at home, Dharmapala entered St. Thomas' College, which included a small all-male high school. I wondered why he persisted in attending Christian schools when his Buddhist orientation invariably led him into difficulties there. While in Sri Lanka, I learned from anthropologist Gananath Obeysekera that, during that time, temple-based schools had lacked academic rigor, because most of the monks were educated primarily in Buddhist teachings. He also told me about the law passed in the 1870s, requiring all children to go to missionary-run schools. Dharmapala's father had greater ambitions for his eldest son than the religious life, and insisted that his education be as rigorous as possible.

At St. Thomas's, Dharmapala encountered the same problems he had in previous schools. The headmaster, Warden Miller, was known for his strictness and use of corporal punishment. Dharmapala came to know it well. When he went to the warden's office one day to request a day off from school, he enraged the man. It was *Vesak*, Dharmapala explained, the day for remembering the birth, enlightenment, and death of the Buddha. The headmaster was astonished that Dharmapala had even asked and exclaimed he would certainly not grant a school holiday for the observance of a Buddhist festival. Dharmapala picked up his books and left school for the rest of the day. The next day he was caned for his impudence. Nevertheless, he did the same thing for the next three years of his tenure at St. Thomas's. Each *Vesak*, Dharmapala would go to Kotahena, a modest Buddhist temple near his parents' home instead of to school. The next day he would endure beatings from the headmaster. However, Kotahena temple was a welcoming place and it became an important site for Dharmapala in shaping his young life and cementing his relationship with his Buddhist ancestry.

He began to skip Sunday School at St. Thomas's to attend services at Kotahena, but he asked his friends to pose questions to the Christian priests about various issues that troubled him. Despite his critical, outspoken ways, he graduated first in his class, and the priests took pride in his knowledge and understanding of Christian theological texts.

While still at St. Thomas's, Dharmapala would walk by the Kotahena temple everyday, sometimes dropping in after school to listen to a Buddhist priest who gaining a name for himself. The priest, Mohattiwatte Gunananda, in a courageous move for those times, critiqued the religion of the missionaries to all who would listen. His lectures were the first public and informed articulation of criticism against centuries of Christian domination. Mohattiwatte soon gained a large following of Buddhists and others who were anxious to hear his talks. When Christian authorities learned of his lectures, they organized a large public meeting in Panadura, near Colombo, in August of 1873. They challenged Mohattiwatte and the scholarly Buddhist priest Venerable Hikkaduwe Sri Sumangala to participate in an open debate with Christian theologians. The debate lasted three days with Mohattiwatte speaking, and Sumangala furnishing the scholarly research. The Buddhist monk was so eloquent and skillful that most of the 10,000 people who witnessed the debate declared that Mohattiwatte was the victor. The Christian missionaries never conceded defeat, and the event was forever after called the Panadura Controversy. Today, every child in Sri Lanka knows the story of the Panadura event, because it peacefully shifted the place of Buddhism back into a central position in the religious life of the Sinhalese people. People were no longer afraid to worship at Buddhist temples and to offer flowers and money at roadside altars.

Theosophy in Sri Lanka

In 1876, Venerable Mohattiwatte received a letter from America congratulating him on his success in the Panadura debate. Dharmapala tells us in his "Reminiscences" that a Dr. J.M. Peebles, an American Spiritualist who was visiting Colombo at the time of the debate, read the proceedings in the *Ceylon Times*. Upon his return to the United States, Peebles shared this document with Henry Steel Olcott and Madame Helena Petrova Blavatsky who had just organized the Theosophical Society in New York. It was Olcott who wrote the Buddhist priest, and the two began a correspondence about what he and Blavatsky claimed to be "psychic relations" with ascended Himalayan masters and their relationship to the Buddha. The Theosophical teachings and revelations had been garnering a large following in America, and huge numbers of people gathered to hear Blavatsky and Olcott. The ascended masters they spoke of were supposedly devoted to the Buddha, and their teachings seemed very familiar and appealing to Mohattiwatte. He received a two-volume book from Olcott entitled *Isis Unveiled,* which he set about translating into Sinhala, the predominant language of Sri Lanka. Soon Mohattiwatte, himself, began lecturing on the text and claimed a relationship between the Theosophical Society and Sinhalese Buddhism. Dharmapala became enamored of the text as well, seeing it as a new way of rendering Buddhist teachings in a modern vernacular. He attended Mohattiwatte's lectures regularly and began assisting the Buddhist priest on his travels around the island and learning as much as he could about the new teachings.[4].

In 1880, Madame Blavatsky and Colonel Olcott visited Sri Lanka, disembarking in the port city of Galle in the South. One of their first actions was to officially become Buddhist, in a ceremoney called 'taking refuge.' This endeared them to the Sinhalese people, and Dharmapala found himself charmed. In his "Reminiscences" he wrote of the experience: "I remember going up to greet them. The moment I touched their hands, I felt overjoyed. The desire for universal brotherhood, for all the things they wanted for humanity, struck a responsive chord in me. I began to read their magazine and everything they had written. As I walked in the gardens overgrown with fragrant plants or along the shore shaded by teak and coco palms, I pondered the conversations I had had with the two Theosophists."[5]

Dharmapala's father was not so enamored of his son's spiritual aspirations, and worried for his son's material future. He encouraged Dharmapala to join the Government and do something practical. Although Dharmapala was entranced by Blavatsky and Olcott, he obeyed his father and was soon hired by the National Department of Education. He worked as a researcher and helped to write educational policy. He was easily promoted several times and proved to be a hard worker. In some way, he felt he was still dedicated to the good of fellow human beings by his work there.

In 1884 Madame Blavatsky and Colonel Olcott again visited Colombo, on their way to Madras, and Dharmapala begged his father to allow him to travel with them to India. After great hesitation, his father consented but on the day of their departure, he announced that he had had a very bad dream and would not permit Dharmapala to go after all. Dharmapala's grandfather was consulted, and he too, opposed the trip. Then the Head Priest, Sumangala, agreed with the family, based on the inauspicious signs and their opposition. Finally, Olcott agreed that he would not take Dharmapala given their objections. Suddenly, Madame Blavatsky arrived and announced: "That boy will die if you do not let him go. I will take him with me and protect him." In the end, the family gave in and Blavatsky, Olcott, and Dharmapala left that day for Adyar, near Madras in south India.[6]

After several months in India, Dharmapala was having difficulties with the Theosophical texts and organization. Madam Blavatsky called Dharmapala to her and told him: "It will be much wiser for you to dedicate yourself to the service of humanity through Buddhism. Return to Colombo, learn Pali, the sacred language of the Buddha, and help to revive the spiritual tradition of your people." Dharmapala was relieved and returned to Sri Lanka, immediately turned his attention to studying the Pali scriptures of early Buddhism, thus, began his work of re-inscribing Buddhism in his homeland. Without evidence, we cannot know what transpired during those months in Adyar, but apparently

Dharmapala recognized his path as Buddhist, rather than Theosophist. Newly energized and focused, he returned to Sri Lanka and began his work in earnest, renewing his commitment to revitalizing Buddhism in Sri Lanka. His primary interest in Theosophy had shifted to its parallels with Buddhism.

In 1885, after he returned from Adyar, the twenty-one-year-old Dharmapala wrote to his father and asked permission to leave the family home and become an *anagarika*, a spiritual seeker without the comforts of home. He requested permission of the Theosophical Society to stay in their headquarters in Colombo to facilitate his study and work on Buddhism and Theosophy. In 1886, Colonel Olcott and C.W. Leadbetter, one of the early forces in the Theosophical Society, went to Sri Lanka where Dharmapala joined them for several months in traveling around the island in a double-decker traveling cart. Consequently, he began to see his country in a very different light, that is, through the eyes of foreigners. Dharmapala learned much about the conditions of his people during that time, and he vowed to promote both Buddhism and Theosophy throughout the country, as well as offer physical and spiritual sustenance to those who were suffering.

During one of his tours with Olcott and Leadbetter, Dharmapala learned that he had been promoted to a higher position in the National Department of Education. It was then he decided to devote his life to Buddhist practice and work. He declined the government position and continued traveling the countryside with his companions. They talked with people about the revival of Buddhism. Along the way, he started a free weekly magazine called *The Buddhist.* He helped to establish Buddhist Sunday schools and offered to distribute Olcott's *Buddhist Catechism* after having it translated into Sinhala.

Dharmapala traveled to Japan with Colonel Olcott in 1890. He carried with him a letter from the head priest in Sri Lanka offering greetings to the Buddhists of Japan. It was the first interaction of Theravada Buddhists with Mahayana Buddhists in more than a thousand years. It was a momentous occasion, and the Japanese celebrated Olcott and Dharmapala all over Japan. Buddhists from differing lineages hosted the two visitors and held meetings about the teachings and the changes that had occurred as Buddhism traveled across the Silk Road from the first century C.E. onward.[7] Dharmapala recorded some of those discussions in his diaries and remarked how different some of the practices of the Mahayana Buddhists were from his own Theravada Buddhism. He acknowledged, nonetheless, how the foundational teachings had remained intact throughout its movement across Asia.[8]

Dharmapala and Olcott remained in Japan for several weeks and then traveled on to India. That second visit changed the direction of Dharmapala's life, and gave him a quest that was to occupy much of his thought and energies for the rest of his life. When he visited Sarnath, the site of the Buddha's first teachings, with members of the Theosophical Society and saw the ruins of that sacred site, he felt as if he should do something to honor the place where the Buddha first taught. Also, when he visited Bodh Gaya, the site of the Buddha's awakening, he felt even more moved to revitalize that sacred site, which had fallen into disrepair and neglect. In his diary, he recorded:

January 22, 1891

After taking breakfast we traveled by train from Sarnath to Buddha Gaya—the most sacred spot to the Buddhists. After driving six miles from the train station in Gaya, we arrived at the holy place. Within a mile, you could see lying scattered here and there broken statues of our blessed Buddha. At the entrance of the (Hindu) Mahant's temple, on both sides of the portico there are statues of the Buddha in the attitude of meditation and expounding the Law. How elevating! The sacred Vihara (temple)! I solemnly promised that I would stop here until I can make sure that Buddhist monks will take charge of this place.[9]

That sentiment did not prove to be as easy as Dharmapala had hoped. The quest to save Bodh Gaya was to plague him for the rest of his life. Dharmapala did remain in Bodh Gaya for some time and attempted to convince the Hindu priest residing there that the site was as sacred to Buddhists as the priest insisted it was for Hindus. After great resistance and negativity from the priest,

Dharmapala embarked on a journey to The Archaeological Survey of India, the British overlords, and finally to Mary Foster.

Realizations from that journey set the direction for the remainder of his life. Engaging many people along the way, Dharmapala deepened his understanding and commitment to transforming Bodh Gaya into a shared site of devotion for both Buddhists and Hindus.

Chapter Four

BODH GAYA, INDIA

B odh Gaya is the site of the awakening of the historical Buddha. Today it is a dusty little village on the Ganges Plain of North India originally inhabited by Hindus, later occupied by Muslims, then Buddhists, and now overrun by tourists, both spiritual and secular.[1] People mostly coexist peacefully, and there is respect for the pilgrims and residents of all faith traditions who come to worship in their respective ways. Buddhist temples have dominated the landscape for the past fifty years or so, but the history of the village is much older and more interesting than its latest incarnation. Anagarika Dharmapala and, by extension, Mary Foster were responsible for certain historic developments in Bodh Gaya, both in governance and in its revitalization as a sacred Buddhist site. From Dharmapala's first visit until his death, Bodh Gaya held a special place in his heart and dominated most of his spiritual attention.

I first encountered Bodh Gaya in 1996, teaching Buddhist Studies for Antioch University. The program began in 1973 and continues to attract students and professors from all over the world. The students come for a variety of reasons—academic, personal, cultural. An immersion program known for its academic and spiritual rigor, it is unique in the way it introduces students to Buddhism. Students are engaged in a variety of spiritual practices, including meditation, visualization, chanting, walking, sweeping the courtyard and other domestic chores—pursuits intended to open and engage their minds. Students are also taught theory and philosophy of Buddhism. Students and faculty members meditate twice a day, with guidance from meditation masters from the Theravada, Mahayana, and Vajrayana traditions. The courses explore the history and movement of Buddhism in time and space. They contextualize the various schools and traditions of Buddhism across many different cultures.

Theravada is the oldest form of Buddhism from the fourth century B.C.E.; it was followed by Mahayana, which developed around the first century C.E. in mostly East Asian countries, and Vajrayana around the sixth century C.E. in Tibet, Sikkim, and India. The three constitute the major streams of Buddhism; each stream contains many schools within. They differ in emphasis and practice, but all subscribe to the foundational teachings of the Buddha: The Four Noble Truths, the Eightfold Path, karma, and rebirth.

In 1996, I joined the Antioch program to teach the Anthropology of Buddhism– its rituals, symbols, semiotics. Traveling with the students from London to the program's site, we arrived midday in nearby Gaya, wilted from the late August climate, steamy and enervating. Our bus bumped along the uneven road shared with cows, water buffaloes, cars, motor rickshaws, push bikes, and people walking from the train station. It took twenty minutes to move the six miles from Gaya to Bodh Gaya along the Naranjana River where the Buddha walked.[1] Our bus moved slowly through the forests where the Buddha resided before his awakening, past timeless small villages with simple thatched-roofed mud huts.

As we neared Bodh Gaya, I was stunned to see the degree of poverty in the village. The houses in town squeezed among the newer Buddhist temples and mosques were mostly hovels. There were a few substantial homes, but it was primarily a village of poor people who barely made a living by serving foreigners. Bodh Gaya had not always been so impoverished. According to accounts in the early sutras, when the Buddha was there, it was forested and beautiful. The texts describe the Naranjana River as flowing with clear, cool water, abundant with fish; it was a place inviting to ascetics and spiritual wanderers. Now the river is muddy, and there is a modern bridge that was built by some Japanese who were able, by some genius and a lot of money, to convince the local authorities to make it easier to cross to the village of Sujata and the caves of Mahakala.

Sujata is named for the village girl who offered milk rice to the Buddha during his aescetic period, when he was in danger of starvation from subsisting on a diet of nettles and one grain of rice each day. She had found him nearly unconscious. and so emaciated that she spoon-fed and revived him. Many stories tell his subsequent realization that there must be a more balanced way to seek awakening. So he moved to a shady fig tree nearby, sat beneath it and began to meditate. The energy that Sujata's milk rice gave him allowed him to gain the insight needed for his full awakening on that spot. Today, pilgrims find their way to her village to honor the memory of that event and her selfless act of generosity. The Mahakala Caves, also across the river, are a series of three caves in which the Buddha was said to have spent a good deal of time meditating and fasting before he decided against extreme ascetic practices. We know from sutras dating back to the third century B.C.E. that that very spot in Bodh Gaya became a pilgrimage site even during Buddha's life. Thanks largely to the friendship of Dharmapala and Mary Foster, it remains so today.

The Buddhist Emperor Asoka

Walking down the road from the Burmese monastery, past tailors and food stalls, dry-good shops and farmers with their produce laid out on burlap bags, I headed toward the Great Temple, the Mahabodhi, to join others in circum-ambulating the tree and the surrounding temple gardens. It is said that the Buddhist Emperor Asoka built the temple around 250 B.C.E. The temple was placed next to the Bodhi tree under which Buddha, Sakyamuni, sat. The preservation of that fig tree and the temple became symbols of the respect that Asoka felt for the Buddha. Asoka had once been a fierce warrior, habitually demolishing whole villages in his quest for greater power. However, after one particularly devastating battle, the Battle of Kalinga, when Asoka surveyed the bloodied battlefield he was suddenly stricken with such horror at the loss of life, that he decided to eschew bloodshed for the rest of his life.

He became a Buddhist, and proclaimed his newly peaceful rule by creating Stone Pillars with edicts carved on them. The edicts were Buddhist rules of conduct and governance for the people, and they earned Asoka the title of *Dharmaraja,* King of Righteousness. The most famous of the rock pillars is in the museum at Sarnath, where Buddha first taught the Dharma. An exquisitely carved lion serves as its crowning feature. Asoka's lion obelisk is now India's national symbol and is respected by all Indians regardless of religion.

Asoka's rule was legendary in India, and many of his inscribed pillars still stand at sacred sites around the country. His governance became informed by his Buddhist beliefs. Asoka also chose the *Dharmachakra*, the Buddhist Wheel of the Law, as his royal symbol, and it too is now a national emblem of India. Asoka incorporated the Buddhist teachings into his daily rule, and his motto became "conquest through *dharma.*" *Dharma* is variously translated as "truth," "teachings," and generally, as "phenomenon." In this instance, it is referring to the Buddhist teachings. Asoka is beloved by Indians to this day as an example of enlightened leadership.

There are numerous stories about the temple that Asoka built in Bodh Gaya. One of the most famous involves Asoka's wife who, it seems, became so jealous of her husband's fascination with Buddhism that she ordered the Bodhi Tree to be chopped down.[1] Fortunately, some years before, Asoka had sent his son Mahinda and his daughter, Sanghamitta, as religious ambassadors to Sri Lanka because the king of Lanka had requested to learn more about the new philosophy called the Buddha's Middle Way. Asoka had included as gifts of state some of the Buddha's relics and a cutting from the original tree. Sri Lanka now boasts the oldest extant tree from that original one in Bodh Gaya. Pilgrims always try to find seeds and leaves that fall from that tree. It is considered auspicious to keep them as mementos or amulets. A cutting from that tree in Sri Lanka was taken back to Bodh Gaya and planted in the place where the original tree stood. Also, a cutting was carried to Honolulu by Dharmapala and given to Mary Foster for her own sacred garden. That tree still stands today.

Destruction of the Temple

The destruction of the original Mahabodhi Temple occurred around 1200 C.E. at the hands of Muslim invaders who were intent on destroying non-Muslim religions. They arrived in India from Turkey and began systematically destroying holy places, particularly those of the Buddhists who were one of the most influential religious groups in India. The Turkic-Muslims felt that the Buddhists might undermine their project of religious conquest, and they therefore set about supplanting it with the teachings of Islam. During their destruction of the Mahabodhi Temple, the iconoclastic Muslim invaders muti-lated the sculptures by cutting off the noses and quite often the heads of the images. Scholars believe the statues were destroyed or defaced because of the Islamic aversion to iconographic representations of God and their mistaken belief that the Buddhists worshipped the statues as divinities.

Such destruction, however, occurred not only in Bodh Gaya, but also at the site of the magnificent university at nearby Nalanda where monks, nuns, and lay scholars had been studying Buddhism since the fifth century C.E. Not only was Nalanda one of the oldest universities in recorded history, it was also an architectural masterpiece with lakes and parks on the campus, and a large library where the old scriptures and commentaries were meticulously copied. It was said that ten thousand students and two thousand teachers were killed at the time of the Muslim destruction of Nalanda in the early years of the thirteenth century.

Some years later, in 1234, a Tibetan monk named Dharmasvamin journeyed to Nalanda and then to Bodh Gaya and wrote that he found the Mahabodhi Temple in great disrepair and attended by a handful of Hindu priests. For some reason, the Hindus were spared the wrath of the Muslim invaders and were allowed to continue their spiritual practices. After that time, Bodh Gaya ceased to be a pilgrimage destination for Buddhists until 1515 when a Burmese mission came.[3] There is no record of other pilgrims or visitors until 1874 when King Mindon of Burma, the great Buddhist monarch, sent a group of monks and skilled carpenters and builders to repair the temple.

Much like Anagarika Dharmapala, King Mindon felt compelled to recover Bodh Gaya for Buddhists and to restore its holiest site. The Burmese met with resistance from the *Mahanta* (Hindu Priest) who had completely taken over the ruins of the temple and dressed the Buddhist statues in Hindu colors and scarves. The Mahanta informed Mindon, as he later did Dharmapala, that Buddhists had no place there and that it was now the Mahanta's property.

In 1891, when Anagarika Dharmapala visited Bodh Gaya for the first time, beginning his lifelong quest to resurrect and reclaim the sacred site for Buddhists, he recalled his first impression of the temple in ruins:

"I was filled with dismay at the neglect and desecration about me. I had intended to stay a few weeks and then return to Ceylon. But, when I saw the condition of the shrine, I began an agitation to restore it to Buddhist control. I communicated with the leading Buddhists of the world and urged them to rescue Bodh Gaya from the Shiva-worshipping Hindus. On May 31, 1891, I started the Maha Bodhi Society, to rescue the holy Buddhist place and to revive Buddhism in India." [4]

It was Dharmapala's intention to devote himself to the restoration and return of the Mahabodhi temple to Buddhists. In 1892, he started publishing the *Maha Bodhi Journal*. He sent it all over the world, to seek help from Buddhist organizations and individuals to restore Bodh Gaya. The journal published articles about philosophical issues in Buddhism and offered readings from various Buddhist texts. He also wrote about his ongoing struggle to save the temple. One of the recipients of the journal was a Dr. John Henry Barrows, the chair of the World's Parliament of Religions that was to be held in Chicago at the World's Columbian Exposition and World's Fair in 1893. Dr. Barrows was so impressed with the journal and its eloquent writer that he invited Dharmapala to be on the advisory council for the Parliament and to find a delegate from the Buddhist tradition in South Asia to attend the event. Dharmapala agreed and approached several of the leading Buddhist scholar-monks, but all felt they were too old to make the journey to Chicago. When Dr. Barrows learned of it, he wrote to Dharmapala, "You come yourself as the delegate to the Congress." Dharmapala wrote in his diary:

I was only twenty-seven at the time, and I did not consider myself qualified to take the place of such a venerable bhikkhu (monk) as should have represented our Sinhalese Buddhists. But I could not disappoint the amiable Dr. Barrows; so I went, in the white robes of a Buddhist student, to the white city that the people of Chicago had built near Lake Michigan to commemorate the discovery of America by Columbus four hundred years before. [5]

With a sense of great responsibility and gratitude to Dr. Barrows, Dharmapala reluctantly embarked upon this journey, not knowing how much it would change his life. The Parliament and Dharmapala's participation in it had a tremendous impact on the young Sri Lankan and ultimately led him to Mary Foster in what would become a remarkable relationship for both of them. She became not only his benefactor, but also his closest friend and he came to refer to her as "my foster mother." He became her teacher, friend, and spiritual guide for the rest of her life.

Bodh Gaya became Dharmapala's passion, and he returned to the dusty village many times during his life thanks to the support of Foster. He had begun his quest to refurbish the temple by meeting with the Mahanta there, but to no avail. He later contacted the Archaeological Survey of India, located in Simla, but that, too, disappointed the young man. The Archaeological Survey, which had been founded in 1861 by Sir Alexander Cunningham and Viceroy Cannin under the British Colonial Government, had as their mission "to uncover and conserve ancient civilizations in India and Afghanistan." When Dharmapala made his request to them for help, they regretted that they could not be of assistance because they were already struggling with the Hindus in India and did not want to alienate them. Later, when Gandhi was beginning his resistance in South Africa exacerbating tensions in India, the British refused to help. Dharmapala reluctantly accepted this official lack of support, and reached out to Buddhists all over the world to ask for their assistance in his endeavor.

His journey to Chicago opened doors that eventually led to restoring Bodh Gaya as a pilgrimage site for Buddhists and all spiritual seekers. Dharmapala insured a Buddhist presence in the management and protection of the temple. Little did he know when he left Colombo for Chicago that the Parliament would bring him significantly closer to realizing his dream, thanks to new associations with spiritual seekers and influential people from many countries, and eventually to Mary Foster.

Chapter Five

CHICAGO

In July of 1893 Dharmapala left Bodh Gaya for Colombo to visit his family and the Venerable Sumangala before setting off to Chicago in September. In September 1993, I attended the 100th anniversary of that same World Parliament of Religions in Chicago.[1] The original Parliament was held as part of the World's Columbian Exposition, a 400-year anniversary of Christopher Columbus's exploits. The Palmer House, the site of both original event and the anniversary, had a grandeur matched only by the parade of religious leaders and practitioners from across the world. There were Hindu *sadhus,* cave-dwellers, witches, and warlocks sitting among rabbis and Imams, archbishops and Zen priests. It was a delight. The array of robes, turbans, and religious paraphernalia assembled in the great lobby of the hotel was a visual feast. There were daily talks and panels, Sufi dancing and yoga, Native American rituals, liturgical music from Christian hymns to Chinese Buddhist Pure Land chants, and a panoply of religious attire, regalia, and ritual.

There Anagarika Dharmapala first encountered the name Mary Foster, and there that his path became intertwined with hers for what would become a lifelong friendship. It was also there that the young Sri Lankan was introduced to a world of spiritual adherents and seekers, with as much faith and enthusiasm for their spiritual search as Dharmapala had for his. Many at the Parliament had never heard anything about Buddhism, and Dharmapala delighted in sharing the philosophy with anyone who might ask.

Richard Hughes Seager, who wrote the most definitive study of the Parliament of Religions of 1893, acknowledged that: "The 1893 Parliament deserves a central place in American and modern religious history. A seventeen-day-long assembly held in September 1893, it was considered by its organizers and those who attended it, as the most noble expression of the World's Columbian Exposition."[2] It was the most noble expression of religious multiplicity and tolerance that the world had ever seen.

The 1893 Parliament was a complex event. There were representatives of many religious traditions—Protestants, Jews, Catholics, Orthodox Syrian, Armenian, Russian, and Greek, scholars in the scientific study of religion and religious history, leaders and practitioners from what were then considered all the "great religions." There were also representatives from Asia and Africa, many of whom introduced the world to previously unknown religious ideas and practices.

The informing spirit of the Parliament was universalistic and liberal and, according to its organizing group, "a meeting that was more widely representative of peoples, nations and tongues than any assemblage ever before convened." It was designed to create a forum for dialogue among religions from across the world. Seager notes that, "the organizers of the Parliament saw the dominant culture of nineteenth century America as embodying a new Greece or Rome…and the most highly evolved and enlightened civilization in history."[3] The vision that America had of itself, and the myth that surrounded the event—America as the new Greece—was deftly challenged during the Parliament by eloquent speakers from Asia and Africa.

The Parliament was conceived at the closing decade of the nineteenth century when millennial predictions and dreams of a liberalizing pluralism in the world were prevalent. It was a time of both hopefulness and doomsday fears. It was a time of technological innovation and increasing colonial conquest. The role of women was being challenged, broadened, and reimagined; civil and human rights were being reformulated. Spiritual longings and discoveries were abundant during that period, with many people reconsidering their own spiritual beliefs and civil practices.[4]

One important liberator movement in India was seeded in 1893 when Mohandas Gandhi encountered social injustice on a train in South Africa, and committed his first act of civil disobedience by refusing to vacate a first-class compartment. That led to his activism on behalf of oppressed people everywhere. The development of his consciousness from that time propelled him onto the world stage and changed the course of his life and the lives of many in India and the world over.

At that time also, Grover Cleveland had been elected for his second term of office and was overwhelmed with financial and political crises at home. One of his major challenges was dealing with the illegal overthrow of the Hawaiian Kingdom that had just occurred. On January 13, 1893, U.S. Marines had landed in Honolulu aboard the USS *Boston* to prevent Queen Liliʻuokalani from abrogating what was called the Bayonet Constitution. On January 17, the queen was illegally deposed, and the Kingdom of Hawaiʻi forced into became a 'republic.' When the treaty came up for approval in Washington, Cleveland was president and retracted it on March 4, 1893. He then launched an investigation into the overthrow, appointing James Henderson Blount as chief investigator. He sent Blount to Hawaiʻi to report on the circumstances surrounding the illegal takeover. The Blount Report stated that the provisional government had not been established with the consent of the Hawaiian people. It also claimed that Liliʻuokalani, fearing a bloody conflict, only surrendered after being told that the provisional government was supported by the United States. According to Blount, the queen was told that the U.S. president would consider her case after her surrender. After reviewing the report, Cleveland decided not to approve the treaty. Blount's findings were then disputed by the provisional government in Hawaiʻi. Cleveland had met the queen in 1888 when she was still a princess and had great respect for her, and supported the reinstatement of the monarchy.

In a message to the U.S. Congress on the Hawaiian question, delivered on December 1893, Cleveland stated to the opposing members:

I suppose that right and justice should determine the path to be followed in treating this subject. If national honesty is to be disregarded and a desire for territorial expansion or dissatisfaction with a form of government not our own ought to regulate our conduct, I have entirely misapprehended the mission and character of our government and the behavior which the conscience of the people demands of their public servants.[5]

Native Hawaiians, who strongly opposed annexation, also organized protests in response to annexation attempts. They rallied behind two groups: Hui Aloha

`Āina (Hawaiian Patriotic League) and Hui Kālai`āina (Hawaiian Political Association). Mary Foster contributed great sums of money to support both organizations. She and her sister Victoria were active in the protests, working behind the scenes to build support and circulate updates on the action. On January 5, 1895, the Hawaiians staged an armed revolution but the attempt was thwarted by supporters of the Republic of Hawai'i, a group consisting of mostly white businessmen and missionary descendants. Those leading the revolution were jailed along with Lili'uokalani who was accused of supporting them.

William McKinley became the next president of the United States in 1897. He favored annexation and signed a new treaty of annexation that was sent to Congress for approval. In response, the two dissenting Hawaiian organizations petitioned Congress to oppose the annexation treaty. In September and October, Hui Aloha `Āina collected a 556-page petition with a total of 21,269 signatures of Native Hawaiians—or over half of native residents — opposing annexation. Hui Kālai`āina collected around 17,000 signatures for restoring the monarchy, but their version has been lost to history. Together, the two groups represented nearly all Native Hawaiians living in Hawai'i.

After presenting the petition to the U.S. Senate and then lobbying senators, the organizers were able to force the treaty's failure in 1897. Unfortunately, in 1898, Congress passed the Newlands Resolution, which resulted in Hawai'i's being annexed for use as military base.[6]

The self-promotion of the United States intended for the Parliament and Exposition was challenged by some of the greatest religious thinkers of the day, both Eastern and Western. Western critics included Joseph Henry Allen, a well-known scholar and editor of the *Unitarian Review*. The Eastern luminaries and critics at the 1893 event included the charismatic Hindu Swami Vivekananda from India, the Zen priest Shaku Soen from Japan, His Royal Highness Chandadat Chutatdahr, a Buddhist prince from Siam, and the Theravadin Buddhist master Anagarika Dharmapala from Sri Lanka. The elegance of those visionaries, inspired by liberal ideals and conversant with

Western ways, brought the Parliament to an unexpected level of spiritual engagement. The participants from Judeo-Christian backgrounds were unprepared for and unaware of the richness of the Eastern traditions, and welcomed, but also questioned, the new knowledge.

The Asian participants shared a broad religious and political agenda for the modernization and vitalization of the East, and endeavored to secure a place in the global ecumenical conversation that began in Chicago. Their papers reflected not only a confidence in the validity of their traditions, but also an eloquence and ability to inspire audiences in English. Not surprising, those who lived in cultures colonized by England were the most easily understood. The two delegates most applauded and feted after the conference were Vivekananda and Anagarika Dharmapala.

Vivekananda was charismatic and appealing. Although he was at the time an obscure Bengali ascetic, he became a favorite with the press and the audiences of the Parliament. John Henry Barrows, the chronicler of the event, recalled that: "When Vivekananda appeared in his ochre robes and turban, greeting the audience as his sisters and brothers in America, he received several minutes of tumultuous applause."[7] The *Daily Inter-Ocean*, a Chicago magazine, noted that great crowds of people, most of whom were women, pressed around the doors leading to the Hall of Columbus…for it had been announced that "Swami Vivekananda, the popular Hindoo (sic) monk…was to speak."[8]

Dharmapala also attracted enormous attention, speaking in beautiful English with an accent that recalled to many an Irish brogue. He was the most popular and charismatic representative of Buddhism at the Parliament. The *St. Louis Observer* noted, "With his black curly locks thrown back from his broad brow, his keen, clear eyes fixed upon the audience, his long brown fingers emphasizing the utterances in his vibrant voice, he looked the very image of a propagandist, and one trembled with excitement to know that such a figure stood at the head of the movement to consolidate all the disciples of the Buddha and to spread 'the Light of Asia' throughout the civilized world."[9]

Dharmapala presented a very progressive form of Buddhism that was cast in terms drawn from the nineteenth-century-intellectual mainstream, according to Seager.[10] That appealed to many in the audience as it resonated with a liberal Christianity that was at the time expanding its influence in America and throughout Europe. The teachings of the Buddha that Dharmapala described were "a comprehensive system of ethics and a transcendental metaphysic embracing a sublime psychology both familiar and appealing to many who attended his presentation."[11]

He quoted William Jones, Thomas Rhys Davids, and his friend Sir Edwin Arnold, early translators of Buddhist philosophy into English, crediting them with opening long-hidden archives of Buddhist thought to the West. His keynote speech, "The World's Debt to the Buddha" was enthusiastically received. People gathered around him after his talk and wanted to know more about Ceylon, the religion, and the man.[12] He was accommodating and gentle, appealing especially to the sensibilities of Christian clergy, as well as to the women delegates. He was particularly interested in the clergy and their interpretations of their own religion. He wrote of it in his diaries as "one of the most fascinating aspects of this gathering."[13]

Dharmapala's intention in attending the Parliament was to share his love of Buddhism with the West, as well as to advocate and seek support for the restoration of the site of Bodh Gaya's sacred site. In addition, he hoped to return the governance of that site into Buddhist hands. Dharmapala made a plea in his keynote speech, which was rewarded by several delegates offering their support afterwards. He was invited to stay on after the Parliament and to give a series of talks in the US to publicize his cause more widely. He was hosted all along the East Coast, throughout the Midwest and then the West. During one of those occasions, Dharmapala was introduced to several wealthy, progressive women. They told him of a woman in Hawai'i known for her generosity and openness to many forms of spirituality. They suggested that she might be willing to help him with the Bodh Gaya project. Dharmapala wrote at length in his diary about the promise of a meeting with Mary Foster: *Several people have told me about a Mrs. Mary Foster, a part-native woman living in Hawaii, and I am hopeful that this kind lady will see fit to help me in my quest to save Buddha Gaya.*[14]

Dharmapala quickly sent a telegram to Mary Foster, asking if it would be possible to meet her. His ship, the USS *Oceania*, was scheduled to stop in Honolulu for one day, October 18, on its way to Japan and then on to South Asia. Mary Foster replied that she would be happy to meet the young Sri Lankan. Having already heard from friends on the east coast that the young man was a true and genuine seeker, an honest and trusting soul, she was intrigued and keen to meet Dharmapala. She had no idea what impact that meeting would have on the rest of her life, and his.

Although she was unable to attend the Parliament herself, Foster followed events and developments closely, thanks to her many friends and acquaintances who were present in Chicago. Because she had already begun to explore different spiritual traditions, had traveled widely, and become friends with people throughout the world who were on a similar path, she knew many who had made the long journey to Chicago. She later remarked to Dharmapala how much she missed attending the Parliament, and many times asked him to tell her stories about the event.[15] My own participation one hundred years later was extraordinarily significant. Meeting with His Holiness the Dalai Lama, hearing the talks of such luminaries as Hans Kung, A.T. Ariyaratne, and Daniel Berrigan, allowed me experience in person some of the greatest spiritual minds of our time.

Chapter Six

HONOLULU

Meeting Dharmapala

Dharmapala stood on the bow of the USS *Oceania* as it glided on blue waters over the reef into Honolulu Harbor. The pali (cliffs) of the Ko'olau mountains were visible in the background, verdant green and sensual. The harbor opened before him, and a foghorn sounded a welcome to the ship. The air was moist on the cheeks of the young Sri Lankan.

It was October and a cool breeze blew in the early morning light. Dharmapala spotted Mary Foster standing on the pier. He replaced the photograph of her in his pocket. She was clothed in an ankle-length dress that was the custom of the time. With her modest countenance and elegant attire, she stood out gracefully. For that auspicious meeting, she was accompanied by two fellow spiritual seekers—Dr. Auguste Jean Baptiste Marquez, her good friend and confidante, and a woman who may have been Duchess Marie de Souza Canavarro. The duchess was a great supporter of Foster's activism on behalf of Hawaiian resistance to the illegal overthrow of their country.

Foster and her retinue ascended the gangplank, her long dress billowing in the trade winds. Her gloved hands were proffered and met by his hands folded in prayer, extending out of white robes worn by a dark, slender beautiful man. With a small bow of the head, Anagarika Dharmapala took Mary Foster's hands in his own and they met with joy and recognition of a shared understanding. She offered fresh fruit and fragrant tropical flowers, and he warmly accepted them; their familiarity to the foliage and scents of Sri Lanka were striking.

They found a comfortable place to sit on the deck, while below on the pier, stevedores rolled luggage to families awaiting reunion amid laughter, tears, colorful lei, and soft trade winds. They took tea and talked of mutual friends.

Dharmpala wrote in his diary that morning: "I have arrived in Honolulu Harbour on the morning of October 18, 1893. It is a beautiful day with billowing white clouds cascading over the cliffs of the volcanic peaks. I am finally meeting Mrs. Mary Foster and I am hopeful that this meeting will be of benefit to us both."[1]

What Mary Foster hoped to gain through her meeting with Dharmapala is known only slightly through Dharmapala's diary. He wrote that "Mrs. Foster seemed anxious to speak privately with me and we were finally given some time to be alone."[2] Looking out over Honolulu, Dharmapala mused that it was not unlike his own island home. It was so glorious that he wished to take a walk and stretch his legs, but the short stopover did not allow the time. That wish was fulfilled some years later when he visited Mary Foster for a longer time and could take in the heavenly air, fragrant with frangipani and white ginger, and to stroll with her through the streets of Honolulu.

Dharmapala's diary recorded that, when he and Mary Foster did speak privately that day, they spoke about her "temper," her great anger and sadness that was fueled mostly by the recent events in Honolulu. She spoke of her friend Queen Lili'uokalani and her imprisonment in the Palace. She must have related details about American marines charging 'Iolani Palace and overthrowing the Hawaiian queen. With instructions from missionary businessmen and their lawyers who were intent on "helping" Hawai'i, the American marines placed Lili'uokalani under arrest and confined her in her own palace. They had treated the queen with little respect when she assumed the throne. Her wishes were not heard, her edicts were not heeded, and the illegal governing forces eventually usurped her power and imprisoned her.

There were other issues influencing the overthrow that Mary Foster shared with Dharmapala. The strategic positioning of the Hawaiian Islands in the Pacific appealed to geo-political ambitions of the United States. Hawai'i was perceived as a strategic asset. Threats from Japan and other Asian nations as well as America's desire to control much of the Pacific made the Islands a valuable acquisition. The abundance of natural resources, fertile land and uncrowded waters also made the Islands an important economic resource. Many today opine that the personal desires and ambitions of the men who came to do God's work in the Islands perhaps superseded the concerns of nation and politics, but there is no doubt that the political and economic issues certainly played a part.

Mary Foster's anger about the situation, which she referred to as her "horrible temper," was overwhelming her, and devoted time together to practicing a form of mindfulness meditation called *Vipassana*. Mrs. Foster took to the method quite easily, and Dharmapala wrote in his diary that she seemed to be able to calm herself by it. He presented her with a copy of the *Visuddhimagga* or *Path of Purification*, a fifth-century text by the Indian monk Buddhaghosa. The manual of practical techniques and methods for developing a strong mind and for living an ethical life was the perfect gift for Mary Foster. Dharmapala wrote that she cherished the book and reminded him many times during their years of friendship how important it was to her.

She also told Dharmapala of her own recent loss: "Although it has been four years since my husband Thomas died, the sadness of that loss has not yet subsided."[3] The *Visuddhimagga* gave her comfort and instruction about how to care for her grief and how to transform her suffering into a stronger state of mind. The significance of the gift was far greater than the young Sri Lankan could have imagined.

Dharmapala spoke to Mary at that first meeting of his desire to restore Bodh Gaya and that he likely made a plea to her to help him realize the project. We do know from his diaries and later from the Maha Bodhi Society newsletters that Mary Foster made a promise to Dharmapala that day, which she honored for the rest of her life. Her assistance was put into the form of trusts that were established for the young Sri Lankan and the work of his Maha Bodhi Society. To this day, the trust provides for Sri Lankans in need. She, a woman of the Islands, while unable to change things in her own homeland was committed to making a positive change in the larger world.

Dharmapala listened intently that as Mary Foster shared the story of the Hawaiian queen's overthrow. He was reminded of his own people who had likewise struggled under colonial oppression for hundreds of years. He told her about the loss of his own culture and religion and how he was determined to revive them. She shared stories of her own resistance to the overthrow. She had participated in the Hui Aloha 'Aina's petition to President Grover Cleveland to protest the unlawful overthrow of the Islands.[4] She worked tirelessly with her sister, Victoria, to assist the queen during that sorrowful period. The queen was aware of the machinations of the interim government and she endorsed the petition that was being circulated, and engaged covertly in the struggle for the return of her monarchy. In 1895, Lili'uokalani traveled to the East Coast under the guise of visiting relatives in Boston. It is easy to imagine Mary Foster wanting to accompany her. David Forbes, the imminent scholar who studies the life of the queen tells me she did not, in fact, join Lili'uokalani, but she surely must have considered doing so. The Queen's entourage made its way to Boston and then on to Washington, D.C., to meet with influential people in order to rally support for the Hawaiian people and the cause of the illegal overthrow of the monarchy. If Mary Foster was not with the queen in body, she was certainly there in spirit. She had been instrumental in collecting the signatures for the petition that was presented to the American president. Certainly, she must have been anxious about the outcome of that meeting. Of all the Native Hawaiians alive at that time in Hawai'i, 21,269 signed the petition to President Cleveland and Mary Foster's signature was among them.[5]

When Foster and her companions were called to disembark from Dharmapala's steamer in the late afternoon, the party said its farewells. Dharmapala wrote in his diary that he felt as if it was an auspicious meeting and that something very fortuitous would come of it. He was right. After Dharmapala's ship departed, Mary Foster immediately began designating funds from her vast resources to support him and later to his Maha Bodhi Society. She contributed enormous sums of money and helped in other ways to fulfill Dharmapala's dream of reawakening Buddhism and of giving care to all those who were suffering in South Asia.

Auguste Marques, The Theosophical Society, and The Emergence of the Salon in Honolulu

One of those who accompanied Mary Foster on the day she met Anagarika Dharmapala was Auguste Marques. A great friend and confidante, he introduced Mary Foster to spiritual seekers and paths she had yet not known. He was a world traveler and a highly educated man, and he and Mary Foster remained close for the rest of their lives.

Auguste Jean Baptiste Marques was born on November 17, 1841, in Toulon, France. He was part French, Scottish, Spanish, and English. He had spent his childhood in Morocco, Algiers, and the Sahara Desert while his father was with the French Foreign Legion.[6] Highly intelligent and well educated, Marques completed a course in medicine at the University of Paris. For some unknown reason, his mother begged him not to follow that career path and instead he entered service in the Bureau of Agriculture in Paris. After his mother's death in 1875 when he was thirty-four, he embarked on a world tour that finally brought him to Hawai'i in 1878. He arrived on the Australian ship *City of Sydney* and decided to stay in the Islands. He was a man of many talents and was to accomplish much in his fifty years in Honolulu. He referred to himself as a "Capitalist" but his sense of capitalism was venture, not profit. He began by buying properties in Mānoa Valley and selling small plots to the arriving Portuguese immigrants who had been lured to the Islands by the promise of high-paying positions as luna (managers) on the burgeoning sugar and pineapple plantations. He put in the first artesian well in the Islands on his property and it served all the community in Mānoa Valley. Marques had a special feeling for the Portuguese immigrants, and many of them believed that he was Portuguese. He did whatever he could to assist them and served as the honorary Portuguese consul for many years.[7]

Marques taught music and French at Punahou School while also serving in diplomatic and legislative positions. He went to Russia in 1886 on a diplomatic mission for the then King, David Kalākaua, and served in Kalākaua's legislature from 1890–1891. Because of his aristocratic background, Marques was quite often called upon to entertain diplomats and foreign visitors. At the request of the king, he negotiated with dignitaries on matters of state. Later, he became the Russian consul in Honolulu in 1908, the Panamanian consul in 1909, the French consul in 1910, and the Belgian consul in 1914. He carried out all of those requests with poise and dignity, making all who met him feel comfortable and welcome. He was awarded an Order of Merit from King Kalākaua, mostly for his work on the plight of Native Hawaiians suffering with Hansen's Disease (leprosy). He also received the prestigious Companion of the Royal Order of Kapʻiolani from the King.[8]

Marques, like Mary Foster, had a spiritual hunger and began to explore Theosophy, Transcendentalism, Buddhism, and Brahmanism; he was looking for a personal path. He organized the Theosophical Society in Honolulu assisted by Mary Foster and held its first meeting in 1894. He and Mary recognized the spiritual leaning in each other and they became very close friends. Together they created a salon, much like the salons of Europe that were popular at the time, often inviting speakers from various spiritual traditions, to share their ideas and practices. The salons were held in Mary Foster's home as well as in rooms in Thomas Foster's office building, on Foster Block, in downtown Honolulu. They invited Henry Steele Olcott, the co-founder of the Theosophical Society, to Honolulu to speak in 1901 and it was recorded in the *Pacific Commercial Advertiser* newspaper as a very special and well-attended public event. Some of their meetings were not such large public affairs. Both Marques and Mary Foster had interests in such things as the revival of esoteric ideas of East and South Asia, and Hawaiian huna (healing and spiritual) practices and philosophy and, because these were subjects suppressed earlier by the missionaries, the meetings on those topics were more exclusive and private.

Marques was as daring a person as Mary Foster. He published a piece for the 1887 issue of Thrum's *Annual* on "Music in Hawaii Nei" that boldly included a description of hula that was still forbidden by missionaries at the time. Missionaries had banned the cultural practice as heathen and provocative and were apparently supported by some of those in the royalty who had converted to the Christian faith. Perhaps Marques was emboldened by King Kalākaua's relationship with the Hale Naua Society that strove to revitalize Hawaiian culture in the late 1880s.[9]

Marques challenged the Victorian sensibilities of the white elite in Honolulu and wrote many learned articles on a variety of issues including the importance of Hawaiian values and the revival of native practices. Perhaps the most regrettable of his published articles was on the growing influence of the Chinese immigrants in Honolulu. Originally, he was a part of the Hawaiian Anti-Asiatic Union, but he later denounced the group and apologized for his part in it. He had gained a more tolerant view after becoming deeply interested in and affected by Theosophy and Buddhism.

The Theosophical Society was a spiritual movement established in 1875 by a Russian woman supposedly of noble birth—Helena Petrovna Blavatsky— and an American lawyer and journalist, Henry Steele Olcott, who preferred to be addressed as the Colonel because of his involvement in the American Civil War. Blavatsky was a large, chain-smoking, outspoken spiritualist usually dressed in long black robes bedecked with shawls and baubles. In one account we learn that her father was a Russian soldier who descended from a family of minor German nobles; her mother who came from a more august line was a novelist and early feminist. By the time she arrived in the United States via Paris in 1873, the story Blavatsky told about her life was a mix of fantasy and fact. She claimed to have traveled the world studying with various spiritual teachers, including Sufi *pirs,* Egyptian Kabbalists, voodoo priests, and most important, a Tibetan by the name of Master Morya with whom she apprenticed in the Himalayas for seven years. In a revealing book, *Madame Blavatsky's Baboon,* historian Peter Washington wrote that Blavatsky professed "to have ridden bareback in a circus, toured Serbia as a concert pianist, opened an ink factory in Odessa, traded as an importer of ostrich feathers in Paris, and worked as interior decorator to the Empress Eugenia."[10]

Arriving in New York, she began to establish herself as a medium and clairvoyant. Olcott met her in September of 1875 at a séance she was holding at her apartment on Irving Place in Manhattan. They became immediate companions and fellow seekers. Her intelligence intrigued Olcott, especially her syncretic understanding of Greek philosophy and early Indian philosophical ideas. He was a successful and established man, a member of a three-man board appointed to investigate Abraham Lincoln's assassination, not one who would be prone to spiritual voodoo. At the time, however, many serious and upstanding people were delving deeply into spirituality. The Civil War had created a kind of desperation and hopelessness, and even Mary Lincoln held séances at the White House in an attempt to communicate with her dead son. People were seeking solace and peace in a shaken world.

During the evening that they met, Blavatsky told Olcott of her desire to bring together many of the thoughts she had gathered in her travels about universal wisdom and the human ability to tap into it. Her quest fascinated Olcott and eventually it formed the foundation of the movement they came to call Theosophy, derived from the Greek *theos* and *sophia* meaning "divine wisdom." The emphasis was on mystical experience, the belief in a deep spiritual reality and an interest in occult phenomena. Both Olcott and Blavatsky held the conviction that a universal wisdom exists and that it can be accessed through meditation, prayer, and revelation.

That evening in Manhattan sparked the creation of the Theosophical Society with Olcott becoming president and Blavatsky the secretary. They attracted a wide variety of people, from free thinkers to liberal clergy and an array of spiritual seekers. Even young Thomas Edison joined the Theosophists and was a regular guest at their salons; he wrote about creating a machine to test psychic powers and ways to communicate with the dead.

The society developed a threefold purpose: promoting the brotherhood of man, studying comparative religion, and investigating "the unexplained laws of Nature and the powers latent in humanity."[11]

Blavatsky and Olcott rented an apartment on West Forty-Seventh Street that journalists called "the Lamasery." It was decorated with plush Victorian furniture, Persian rugs, Asian icons and statues, and piles of books and articles. What was most striking was the array of taxidermists' stuffed animals, including a bespectacled baboon in a shirt and tie, holding under its arm a manuscript of a lecture by Charles Darwin. Peter Washington wrote that it stood for "the folly of science as opposed to the wisdom of religion."[12] The Theosophists were not against science; they aimed at a synthesis of religion, science, and philosophy—all of it rooted in the secret wisdom of ancient masters. There was the belief that the scientific method could open supernatural realms to human comprehension.

In 1877, Blavatsky, with the help of Olcott, wrote *Isis Unveiled* wherein they described and clarified their basic understandings of Theosophy. There were three major characteristics of the ancient wisdom that they wrote about: The first characteristic was that human beings devolved from higher realms of spirit and consciousness into matter and are able to re-ascend to a higher state; the second was that ancient civilizations understood the relationship between spirit and science which we have temporarily lost; and the third was that a fraternity of adepts conserved and passed the sacred knowledge to others throughout history. Blavatsky and Olcott gleaned from that knowledge their objectives in creating the Theosophical Society. They proposed the creation of a universal community through comparative study and research of spiritual, philosophical, and psychic ideas of human beings.[13]

By the end of the nineteenth century, there were over six hundred branches of the Theosophical Society around the world. Most people had heard of the movement even if they did not subscribe to its teachings or support its efforts. Blavatsky and Olcott moved the Theosophical Society headquarters to Adyar, India, in 1880 and developed a populist Buddhist anticolonial position. That was the period when they met young Anagarika Dharmapala. They traveled to Sri Lanka to spread their teachings in the same year. Their visit inspired many Sinhalese because of the theosophists' affirmation of the traditional cultures of Lanka and India and the relationship to the Buddha. Olcott's support strengthened the local political and cultural leaders who used Theosophy as an ideological weapon in their struggle to regain self-determination. In Hawai'i, as well, Theosophy offered an alternative to the predominance of Christian sects and established an appreciation of Asian philosophies, which had been introduced by Japanese and Chinese laborers and others.

Auguste Marques was sympathetic and interested in what those Asian philosophies offered. That is what drew him to the Theosophists in the first place. He became the first president of the Theosophical Society in Hawai'i and it was through that connection that he introduced Mary Foster to many people associated with the society around the world. Among those that we know of were two women with whom Mary Foster traveled and collaborated on several Theosophical and Buddhist projects.

Constance Wachtmeister and Marie de Souza Canavarro

The first of Mary's spiritual friends was Duchess Marie de Souza Canavarro, an early Theosophist, and the wife of the Portuguese consul in Honolulu. Mrs. Canavarro was a Roman Catholic who had become disillusioned with the Church and, by the time she and her husband arrived in Hawai'i from California in the early 1890s, she was deeply engaged in an exploration of other spiritual traditions. She met Mary Foster and the two kindred spirits became lifelong friends. She was very active in the Theosophical Society, the Lotus Reading Group, a sub group of the Theosophists, and in the developing Buddhist religion in Honolulu. We know from their correspondence that she worked closely with Mary Foster on several projects and traveled widely with her.[14]

The second connection from the Theosophical Society was Countess Constance Wachtmeister who became another of Mary Foster's close friends. She had married her own cousin, the Count Wachtmeister, with whom she had a son, Count Axel Raoul, (1865–1947) who became a well-known figure in royal circles during his life. Axel Raoul Wachtmeister was also a well-known musical composer in his day. His most outstanding work was, interestingly enough, an opera-oratorio called *Prince Siddhartha*.

After three years of marriage, the Wachtmeisters moved to Stockholm where, in 1868, the count was appointed Minister of Foreign Affairs. After his death in 1871, Constance Wachtmeister continued to live in Sweden for several years until 1881 when she joined the Theosophical Society. She soon became an important collaborator with Helena Blavatsky on one of the most famous treatises of Theosophy called *The Secret Doctrine*. The Countess also wrote *Reminiscences of H.P. Blavatsky and the Secret Doctrine* that is a source for study of the personality of Madame Blavatsky and the creation of the *Secret Doctrine*. She became one of the most famous women in the Theosophical Movement next to Annie Besant. She met Mary Foster in 1890 and the two, according to correspondence among Mary Foster's personal papers in the Archives, may have traveled together to India in 1894. They remained friends throughout their lives and the countess encouraged Mary Foster in her work with Dharmapala and the Maha Bodhi Society. The Countess's name appears in the annals of the Maha Bodhi Society so it is obvious that she had some relationship with the group. It may have been during her travels with Mary Foster that she was introduced to the Society and perhaps to Dharmapala.[15]

Victoria Ward

A third influential woman in Mary Foster's life was her own sister, Victoria Ward, one of her closest confidantes and allies. She participated in Mary's public events and private activities, always offering support to her sister. Together, they worked behind the scenes in the 1895 attempt to save the kingdom. Victoria and Mary were instrumental in gathering signatures for the Petition that was sent to Washington, D.C., to President Grover Cleveland in 1895 and actively supported the queen in every possible way. The two sisters stayed close throughout their lives and Mary Foster moved to Victoria's estate, Old Plantation, and lived out the last five months of her life there, while being assisted by her sister and Victoria's three daughters.

They were all powerful women who were part of a society that did not yet fully recognize their gifts. They never held public office but worked publicly for their causes. They conducted meetings in their homes as well as at Foster Block. Following the salon tradition that was gaining popularity in Europe, it would be fair to conjecture that the women spoke about the upheaval in their land and other issues that mattered at their salon meetings. They were more involved in the political discourse of the day than might have been previously thought. They worked behind the scenes, bringing change not only through their wealth but also through their expansive ideas and considerable global influence. Mary Foster and her companions impacted many things through their words and actions throughout the islands and all over the world. Their work with the Theosophists and their contributions to Dharmapala helped to define the later lives of those remarkable women. Certainly, the young Sri Lankan could not have known that on that October day on the *Oceania* they would have an impact on the rest of his life and he would have a tremendous influence on theirs.

Chapter Seven

THE PURE LAND

Long before this account of Mary Foster's story, part of her life was chronicled in the history of the Honpa Hongwanji Mission of Hawai'i in a publication honoring their 100-year anniversary in Hawai'i. According to the temple history, the Reverend Hōni Satomi had been sent to Hawai'i from Japan in 1898, to officially establish the Jōdō Shinshū sect of Buddhism in the Islands. There had been others before him including genuine priests like Soryu Kagahi. There were also several impostors who, posing as spiritual leaders, embezzled money from the spiritually hungry Japanese plantation workers. Satomi, however, was the first who was endorsed by the head temple in the ancient capital of Kyōto. He stayed for a year, working with local Japanese businessmen and plantation workers to propagate the Buddha's teachings among the Islands' various Japanese communities.[1] He returned to Japan and, when he came again in 1899, he was accompanied by a young priest who had recently graduated from Keio University. The young man's passions were literature and Buddhism. The young priest's name was the Reverend Yemyō Imamura. He was a slender, serious intellectual and his charge was to work with the rough, wildly uninhibited young men on the plantations who were deprived of the company of women and frustrated by the hardship conditions that they were forced to live under in the Islands. They were men who had been sold empty promises, men who had come from a desperate Japan to a rainbow-gilded, sweaty, poisoned indenture. Imamura persevered with the men, often sleeping on the floors of their plantation bunkhouses, and always pleading with them to heed the *dharma*, the teachings of the Buddha.

Meanwhile, at the same time, Bishop Satomi encouraged the local Japanese business community to raise money for a Buddhist temple to support the plantation workers as well as themselves. The temple was needed as a place of spiritual refuge as well as a community center. The enthusiastic businessmen were successful in raising enough money to purchase a 12,500-square foot parcel of land on Fort Lane in downtown Honolulu.

At that time also, Mary Foster became a participant in the project. Members of the Japanese business community had heard of Mrs. Foster's generous donations to Buddhist communities in India and Sri Lanka, and her support for the building of hospitals, schools, and temples. They certainly knew of her business acumen and her family's successful shipping company. A key Japanese businessman, probably Saiji Kimura, from Hilo, approached Mary Foster to explain the intentions of the Japanese Buddhist community. Kimura may have done business with her and her husband and perhaps even with her father over the years. He traveled to Honolulu often on business and for his work with the Department of Immigration as their labor supervisor. He advised the young Bishop to meet with Mary Foster and to gain her friendship and support.

Bishop Imamura met with Mary Foster in 1899 and she gladly responded to the request of the Bishop on behalf of the Japanese community. She gave enough money for the entire temple to be constructed. The completed temple (36 feet wide, 60 feet long) had a peaked roof standing over 40 feet high. It was finished in November of 1900 at a cost of $15,725. Mary Foster was highlighted in a *Pacific Commercial Advertiser* article as one of the honored guests at the dedication ceremony and she was acknowledged there for her generous contribution. Archival references regarding the establishment of the first Buddhist temple in Honolulu always mention her involvement.[2]

Mary Foster and Bishop Imamura developed a deep and lasting friendship and met on many occasions regarding the building of the temple as well as spiritual matters. Mary Foster had been struggling with her own spiritual practice in an environment of liturgical machinations; there is no doubt that she had qualms about the offerings of the established religions in her Islands. She practiced Vipassana meditation on her own and struggled to live a Buddhist life based on the *Visuddhimagga*, the text given to her by Dharmapala.[3] Bishop Imamura wrote of such matters in his diaries: *"Mary Foster has proven to be a true friend of the Hongwanji and the Japanese people and is a deeply spiritual woman."*[4]

Mary Foster cared deeply for Bishop Imamura. And it is interesting to speculate if there was not more that compelled her to support him and the Japanese immigrant community. Could she have felt some kinship with their desire to find spiritual sustenance in the increasingly hostile environment that was controlling the Hawaiian Islands? Was it Buddhism, itself, that inspired her to offer support? Was she merely sympathetic to the Japanese immigrants who were dropped down into an alien environment without the benefit of language, history, and relationships?

It remains unclear whether Mary Foster ever officially become a Buddhist. Many refer to her as a Buddhist, but there is no record of a formal declaration or ceremony except for a request she made to have a Buddhist service for her funeral. The request was neither honored nor fulfilled by her family.[5] Obviously, she was deeply touched by Buddhist philosophical ideas, and by her great teachers, Bishop Imamura and Dharmapala.

It is important to remember the environment in Hawai'i at that time in order to understand her and her family's position. Native Hawaiians were being decimated by disease, the loss of their own spiritual and cultural identity, and the seizure of their land. Haole businessmen and missionaries dominated the political and social landscape. Christianity was the dominating religious force in the Islands. It is possible that Mary Foster felt empathy for the Japanese because of their disenfranchisement from their own land in Meiji Japan and the loss of their own culture as the result of their move to Hawai'i. A look back at the plight of those *Issei* (first generation) men provides insights into the nature of their suffering.[6]

Kalākaua and the Meiji Emperor

King David Kalākaua traveled to Japan in 1881 and met the Meiji Emperor, Mutsuhito. The reasons for his going are pertinent to our story. In just one century of contact with the West, the Native Hawaiian population had plummeted from over 400,000 at the first contact to fewer than 50,000 during

Kalākaua's reign. The King had witnessed death among his people from diseases such as smallpox, cholera, and venereal disease that had been introduced by foreigners. His people also suffered a loss of cultural integrity with the introduction of religious and cultural ideas from abroad. Kalākaua desired to repopulate his kingdom. Also, less importantly perhaps, the sugar industry needed a dependable labor supply at that time. Whether Kalākaua was representing that interest is uncertain. We do know, however, that he yearned for more people to come to his islands. Dennis Ogawa, in *Kodomo No Tame Ni,* mentioned that Kalākaua sensed that the Japanese people were connected to the Polynesian race in blood and genetic background and, thus, he seemed to feel some kinship with them. Geneticists and anthropologists have now confirmed Kalākaua's intuition or belief.[7]

Kalākaua and the Meiji Emperor developed a friendship of mutual respect and at one point, the king even suggested a marriage between the Crown Prince of Japan and Princess Kaʻiulani. That never came to pass but it is very telling that the proposal was considered. Kalākaua proposed emigration of Japanese farmers and others from the depressed areas of Japan and the Emperor suggested Kumamoto on the island of Kyūshū as a possible place to look for a ready labor source. Kyūshū had been the site of the Satsuma Rebellion, an attempt to usurp the Western-oriented Meiji government. The Meiji oligarchy may have been happy to see those people go. Former Samurai warriors in Kyūshū had been upset about the direction in which the country was moving with the beginning of importation of Western ideas and materials. The Samurai felt threatened by the possible dilution of their culture and the loss of their own status. The Meiji Restoration opened Japan to the world after 200 years of isolation and exclusionary cultural development, and many Japanese were eager to learn about and enjoy the changes that were occurring all over the world. That was not so for the Samurai class. They joined with farmers and others who were suffering from natural loss through an unusual drought that had resulted in the diminishing of their own wealth and status. Together they rose up in rebellion against the Meiji rulers. It was a short-lived civil disruption that ended after nine months when the Samurai leader, Saigō Takamori, committed suicide. As a result,

Kyūshū was largely cut off from the benefits of the Meiji restoration. Thus, the Meiji Emperor agreed to allow the people from Kyūshū to travel to Hawai'i as contract laborers. The first contingent arrived in Honolulu in February of 1885 on the ship *Tokio Maru*.[8]

During that time, Kalākaua's power began to wane and the American sugar barons were gaining more influence; as a consequence, the treatment of the Japanese immigrants was not what Kalākaua had promised the Meiji Emperor. Count Inouye, the foreign minister of Japan in Hawai'i had asked Kalākaua not to classify the Japanese laborers as "coolies." However, the Kyūshū laborers were treated very badly and were subjected to racial discrimination and inhumane conditions on the plantations. There was little that Kalākaua could do to remedy their situation.

Mary Foster was well aware of the situation and was sensitive to the horrible conditions of the plantation workers. After all, she knew that most Native Hawaiians had refused to work under those conditions, which had resulted in the importation of labor from Asia. Years before, with the discovery of sandalwood trees in the Islands, Native Hawaiians had been forced to clear cut their forests and transport fragrant wood to Honolulu Harbor; sadly, they watched and mourned as the wood was exported to lands beyond their imaginations. Many of the Hawaiians were distraught because of the loss. Not too many years later, when told they would be working on plantations that would change their land from sustainable ahupua'a (traditional Hawaiian land division) to sugar, they balked and refused the work.[9]

Mary Foster remembered those early days of loss and dissatisfaction and, after learning about the background of the Japanese laborers, vowed to help them as much as she could. She learned that some of them had engaged in the unsuccessful Satsuma Rebellion in 1877 to unseat the Meiji Emperor. Mary Foster, herself, had participated in an unsuccessful attempt to oust the illegal government that had overthrown her queen in 1895, an event that changed the course of her Islands. She most likely identified with the Japanese workers;

although her full motivation in supporting them will never really be known, her actions are recorded in the Honolulu English-language, Japanese-language, and Hawaiian-language newspapers of that time as well as in the archives of the Honpa Hongwanji Temple. In one English-language newspaper account at the time, she was represented as "a businesswoman of means who deigns to help the Japanese community."[10] What a thin slice of her life and such a meagre description of the powerful woman Mary Foster was. It also speaks of misunderstanding her intentions. Blame does not lie with the newspaper journalists; rather, it was the time in which the events took place.

Mary Foster developed a close tie with the Japanese workers and with the temple and offered her assistance whenever asked. Bishop Imamura considered her a good friend of the Japanese Buddhists. She played a significant role in and was invited to the public opening of the temple that she had funded and was given the status of the most honored guest.

Although the temple was completed in December of 1899, the actual public opening of the temple did not occur until the next year (November 25, 1900). Late in December, disaster struck all of downtown Honolulu with the outbreak of bubonic plague in Chinatown, a quarter located very close to the site of the new temple on Fort Street. The work of the priests, Satomi and Imamura, shifted from planning a celebration to helping those made homeless by the disaster. In response to the plague, the Department of Health took a radical approach and quarantined all Asians and burned down their homes. On a particular day, after futile attempts at quarantine, inspection, and disinfection had failed, the health officials ordered fires set. One of the fires roared out of control because of a change in the direction of the wind and all of Chinatown burned to the ground. Thousands of Chinese and Japanese were left homeless and penniless. All of their possessions were consumed by the fire. Imamura wrote about the epidemic and its consequences: *"Centering from the Nuuanu area where the disease was discovered, the entire area from Nuuanu Street to River Street was put to flames and reduced to ashes. The area was then quarantined, guarded and restricted by the police. The desperation and confusion of those living in the area was more than they could bear. Only doctors, newsmen, and clergy were given permission and passes to enter the area. I immediately went to see what I could do, and was overwhelmed by people begging for help…Being the only available minister at the Hongwanji, I became a handy man and from eight in the morning to midnight, I ran errands and helped in every way to tend to the people's needs."* [11]

The devastating conflagration left sixty people dead and many more injured. Thirteen of the deceased were Japanese immigrants. The first service held at the new temple on Fort Lane was a memorial service for those people. Plans for the opening dedication ceremony were put aside for the time. Fifteen hundred Japanese were homeless and in need of help. The temple did its best to aid them, creating a welfare organization called the *Kyōai-kai*, and solicited funds to help in their recovery. Mary Foster gave generously to the organization and encouraged friends and family to give what they could.

At the same time, Bishop Imamura worked tirelessly to help all the Japanese in Honolulu including those who were not affected by the Chinatown incident. He opened a night school to teach them English and organized the first Young Men's Buddhist Association, fashioned after the YMCA model. The young men assisted in the night school activities, volunteering along with several haole, to offer English language and translation services. Among those who offered time and language skills was a Mrs. Ellen Barber, who was a Buddhist practitioner. She and Mary Foster were friends and both of them encouraged Bishop Imamura with his desire to integrate Buddhist ideals into life in Honolulu. He, in turn, was very encouraging to the two women by inviting them to services and meetings at the temple. In fact, at the opening celebration on November 25, 1900, Imamura recollected, "I was so pleasantly surprised that more than one hundred Caucasians attended the service." [12]

Even so, Imamura was not unaware of the resistance to his Buddhist temple among the people in Honolulu and noted that: *"Generally speaking, it can not be said that the acceptance of the Buddhist religion in Hawai'i is enthusiastic. Far from it. Deep problems face the Hongwanji still. It is not for the lack of followers.*

Immigrants from Hiroshima, Yamaguchi, Kumamoto, and Fukuoka comprised an extremely large membership. But they were in a new land and not in Japan. We Japanese Buddhists have come into a Christian country." [13] Imamura realized that it was difficult for the Japanese immigrants who were trying to integrate into the new society. They were hesitant and often wondered if it was really all right to follow the Buddhist path in Hawai'i. Mary Foster offered her assistance to the Bishop on the matter by helping Japanese people feel safe in attending the Hongwanji Temple. She introduced Bishop Imamura to the ideas of Theosophy and invited Henry Steele Olcott, one of the founders of the Theosophical Society, to come to Hawai'i to give a talk at the Hongwanji temple. His talk was entitled "Buddhism, the Superior Religion." As Mary Foster and Olcott were old friends who had been introduced years earlier, Mary had no trouble in convincing Olcott to come out to Honolulu. She hosted the Colonel in February 1901. Olcott's lecture was well attended and the Hongwanji Temple was filled to overflowing. [14]

Imamura wrote about the event:

"I took the opportunity to schedule a lecture by him (Olcott), interpreted by then president of Hawaii Shimpō, Mr. Shiowasa. Olcott orated for well over an hour on the topic of 'Buddhism: The Superior Religion.' Even those who had never entered a Buddhist temple were seen in attendance. The morning newspapers carried a synopsis of the lecture. The discovery that there were serious followers of Buddhism even among the Caucasians lifted the inferior feeling among the Hongwanji members and gradually, the attendance at the temple increased. Thus, no longer in shame, openly and with confidence, membership ascended!" [15]

The local attention given to the Hongwanji became even more widespread after Mary Foster invited Queen Lili'uokalani to a special service honoring Shinran, the founder of the Hongwanji's Jōdo Shin Shū sect. Imamura wrote that he had heard that the queen had some interest in Buddhism and some sympathy and goodwill toward the Japanese people. He told also of his royal connections through Mary Foster and through one of his members, a Japanese gardener who worked for the queen. The gardener had told the bishop that Queen

Lili'uokalani was very friendly to Japanese people. He explained also that, while working in her garden, the queen asked him how the Japanese people were faring. The bishop asked Mary Foster to convey a special invitation to the queen to attend the *Gotanye* service that honored the birthday of Shinran. She accompanied the queen to the service held on May 19, 1901 and, afterward, the Queen Lili'uokalani, Mary Foster, and Dr. Marques were invited to dine with the bishop and the board of the temple.

Because it was the first time that the queen had attended a Japanese event, the publicity was enormous, and Imamura wrote: "Reporters from every land throughout the world telegraphed news of the event in large captions. In Japan, articles appeared in all the newspapers such as the *Jiji Shimpō* in Tokyo and the *Ōsaka Asahi* and the consequence was that the Hongwanji found its self-esteem elevated tremendously."[16]

The Pacific Commercial Advertiser published several long articles on May 20, 1901, the day following the momentous event. One article even included the complete text of Bishop Imamura's talk on Shinran Shōnin. It was the first widespread introduction of Buddhist teachings to the general public in Hawai'i. The publication did much to improve the status of the temple and to diminish concerns about the Buddhist philosophy and the people who were followers of Buddhism.

Mary Foster must have welcomed the display and felt reassured by the reception that the event and the temple received from the general public following the queen's visit. Queen Lili'uokalani wrote in her diary about the event as a "profound spiritual experience."[17] The queen, a devout Christian, perhaps desired to see how Buddhism manifested in the Japanese tradition. Mary Foster had been among a handful of people who were allowed to visit the queen while she was imprisoned in 'Iolani Palace. Surely during her visits, she shared with the monarch how Buddhist meditation and philosophy had helped her with her own grief and anger. Perhaps the promise of a salve for her aching heart propelled the queen to accompany Mary Foster on that spring day.

The New Hongwanji Temple and the School

What followed the queen's visit was an increased membership in the Hongwanji Temple. It soon became obvious that there was a need for a new, larger temple to accommodate the numbers of members and guests. Also, Bishop Imamura desired to build a high school near the temple to increase opportunities for the young Japanese children of plantation workers. He recognized that the Japanese who had originally endeavored to make their money from their contract labor meant eventually to return to Japan. Instead, most had settled in Hawai'i. Because of that, the bishop felt that their children needed to be educated to do more than fieldwork for the sugar companies. Some of the plantation workers did not agree. They told him, "When the need arises for our children to go to higher schools, we will have attained success in our businesses and will have returned to Japan. The children can receive higher education there. Why bother to begin a project at this time when there is no urgent need."[16]

For Imamura, the need was urgent. He realized that many of the laborers would never return to Japan. In 1906, while he was in Japan visiting the Hongwanji abbot, he related his concerns and his wish for the education of the Japanese children in Hawai'i. The abbot was enthusiastic about the idea and offered his support. Imamura wrote about the meeting:

"This unexpected encouragement brought me such inner peace! From this light cast upon my path came a renewal of my determination and resolve. Upon my return to Hawai'i, I went to see Mrs. Mary Foster, a warmly supportive patron in recent years, to explain to her the desire for a new school building. She immediately agreed with my idea and, on the spot, presented me the land for the school. Her graceful figure raising her arms to say, 'this land is yours!' will always remain in my memory. I have never again felt that height of happiness as when first, the encouraging words from the Abbot and then, on this return to Hawai'i, the support of Mrs. Foster. The memory of these experiences continues to overwhelm me with warm gratitude on every occasion."[17]

The land that Mary Foster offered the bishop for the new temple was on Nuʻuanu and Upper Fort Street, as the Pali Highway was called in those days. The road had just been opened up past School Street, bisecting the piece of land that Mary Foster had donated. The area was covered in kiawe trees and taro patches and was farmed by a Chinese man to whom permission had been given by Mary Foster. Mrs. Foster gave the man another substantial piece of land to farm and allowed him time to harvest his taro and move to the new location before the construction of the temple began.

The taro patches had to be drained and the land leveled before the construction of the building. While that process took place, Mary Foster donated more money to Imamura that was then matched by the headquarters of the Hongwanji Temple in Kyōto. With those funds, the bishop was able to transport the school building from the old Fort Lane temple grounds to the new site. The refurbished building became the foundation for the new school and then additional buildings were constructed for dormitories to house the students.

The school opened in September 1907 with ten students, all boys. Two years later, after another dormitory was built, Bishop Imamura welcomed ten girl students to the school. He wrote that he saw no difference between the girls' and the boys' need for education. His progressive viewpoint was unusual for the times and people in Honolulu were amazed by his forward thinking.

Most of the students at the school were from poor plantation workers' families and Imamura raised scholarship money for them. Many of those students became pillars of Hawaiian society including Justice Wilfred Tsukiyama, the first Supreme Court Justice of Hawaiʻi. Japanese people in Honolulu still talk about the importance of the school for their family and community's success.

The haole community in Honolulu was suspicious of the school at first; they were concerned that the education was promoting Japanese nationalism because the Japanese language was being taught. Bishop Imamura assured them that the aim of the school was to "develop the characters of citizens of Japanese ancestry based on the ideal of contributing to the culture of America, nurturing the true understanding of both East and West cultures through education in both English and Japanese languages."[18]

Mary Foster defended Imamura and pointed out that many of the Japanese immigrant community were contributing to the growth of the civic culture of Honolulu. The temple's English Language School was educating literate, enterprising young people who were entering the university and opening businesses in the city. In fact, she said, the Hongwanji school "extended its ready hand" when the local YMCA asked for cooperation in a proposed citizenship education campaign in 1914. Then, as the controversy began about America's entry into World War I, the Hongwanji Hawai'i Betsuin published reprints of five *Great State Papers of American History* with a Japanese translation "to inform our community," Bishop Imamura said, "of the true values and principles of this great Democracy."[19] Much later, the Hongwanji members also volunteered and defended the United States in World War II as soldiers. That story is well known because of the bravery of those men who comprised the 442nd Regiment and the 100th Battalion.[20]

Mary Foster remained a staunch supporter of the Japanese Buddhist temple and of the community throughout her life. When Bishop Imamura wanted to build a larger temple to accommodate all of the new practitioners, he sought out Mary Foster for her advice and guidance. The bishop knew that Mary Foster would give him the best way to actualize the project without provoking the larger community. Together, they designed the temple—with Indian (Gandharan) elements to represent Buddhism's Indian roots, a Japanese altar and implements to represent Shin Buddhist roots, and pews, pulpit, and hymnals to represent the new American form of Buddhism.[21]

The structure was 66 feet high, 80 feet wide, 120 feet deep, and had a 20-foot-high dome capping the roof. The land that Mary Foster originally gave the bishop for the schools in 1907 was so vast and extensive that it could easily accommodate the new, stately temple without necessitating additional land. For the groundbreaking ceremony in July of 1916, a Hawaiian boulder weighing more than a ton was brought to the site on a black lacquer carriage that was supported in the air palanquin-style by members of the temple. On the sides of the carriage were gold engraved letters: *Namu Amida Butsu.* About 400 of the women members, dressed in formal black silk kimonos, held the braided red and white silk ropes attached to the palanquin carrying the boulder from the old temple site to the new one. The men were carrying the palanquin on their backs while the women walked behind, holding the silk cords, symbolically helping the vehicle to progress.[22]

It took two years to complete the temple and the *Honolulu Advertiser* noted: "The building is strikingly beautiful." The article made some comment about the strange implements on the altar but failed to mention the pews and hymnals. The Hongwanji was still fighting an uphill battle for acceptance by the haole community in Honolulu. In July of 1918, the temple was formally dedicated, and Mary Foster was in attendance at the event. Her open interest in Buddhism and support of the Hongwanji Temple, caused some to label her "eccentric."[23] She cared not for those who would try to slander her, and she supported and protected the Hongwanji until her death.

In 1929, Mary Foster invited the famous Sir Rabindranath Tagore, the pre-eminent Indian philosopher and poet, to Honolulu and asked him to give a lecture at the Hongwanji. He spoke to an overflowing crowd, according to the newspapers, and charmed the entire Honolulu community. In fact, whenever a famous religious leader or distinguished scholar of religion was in town, Mary Foster arranged for a lecture or meeting to be held at the Hongwanji Temple. They would have been invited initially to Honolulu by Mary Foster and her friends to participate in the salon that she hosted. Generally she encouraged the visitors to do a public lecture as well in order to offer their wisdom to a wider audience. The Hongwanji Temple benefitted as well by having the larger community visit their temple as a way to see the Japanese part of the community of Honolulu.

Mary Foster remained involved in the Hongwanji Temple for the rest of her life. She is honored there to this day for her compassionate understanding of their struggle and for her undying respect for Bishop Imamura and the *buddha dharma* (the teachings of the Buddha). They also remember her for her resonance with their Buddhist beliefs and philosophy. She gave more than money to fund their projects; she championed their right to enjoy and practice their religion. She also made their acceptance into Honolulu society easier by her ever-present involvement and support of Bishop Imamura and the Honpa Hongwanji Temple.

Chapter Eight

BODH GAYA

While all of the activity was taking place in Honolulu at the Pure Land Buddhist Temple in the early 1900s, Mary Foster was also paying attention to struggles in Asia. Her constant communication with Anagarika Dharmapala kept her apprised of what was happening in Sri Lanka and in India and particularly with Anagarika's struggle in Bodh Gaya. She continually supported his projects, both financially and spiritually, believing that his work had great meaning and would develop into something of value to Buddhists and many others around the world.

I was thinking about his struggles and her involvement as I sat on a makeshift stage at the Mahabodhi Temple waiting for the beginning of what turned out to be a very auspicious event. It was the autumn of 1998. The long light of the early morning sun was already making its presence felt by the hundreds of people gathered for a celebration of Mary Foster and Dharmapala. I was sitting between Venerable Nyaneinda, abbot of the Burmese temple, the most powerful Buddhist monk in Bodh Gaya, and a delightful Buddhist priest the Venerable Mitsuhashi Vipulatissa, abbot of Bodh Gaya's Japanese temple. I was in Bodh Gaya to attend this annual event presented by the Maha Bodhi Society. The society preserved the memory of Mary Foster by presenting an event each September, on or near Mary's birthday on the 21st. I had been asked to give a talk about Mary Foster and her relationship to Bodh Gaya and to Anagarika Dharmapala. I intended to offer something about her life in the Hawaiian Islands as well as how she and Dharmapala met and shared so many things in common.

The Maha Bodhi Society, begun by Dharmapala in 1891, still has a major presence in Bodh Gaya and is regarded as the host organization to pilgrims and other visitors to the sacred temple. The society, as we have already discussed, was formed initially to bring the Mahabodhi Temple management into Buddhist hands after it was lost so long ago to the Muslim invasion (1200 C.E.), and later to a Hindu sect, followers of Shiva, who took over the structure after its abandonment. The struggle for control between the Buddhists and the Shaivites lasted from 1891 to 1951 when a Temple Management Committee was finally created. The committee consists of three Buddhists, three Hindus, and an elected official of the Bodh Gaya district. The constitution of the committee was a compromise not satisfactory to anyone, but it was the solution offered by Prime Minister Jawaharlal Nehru to resolve the sixty-year battle for control.

There were actually three groups that had laid claim to Bodh Gaya—the priestly caste-based community of Gayawals, the Saivite Giri monastics of Bodh Gaya, and the Buddhist Maha Bodhi Society that had been spearheaded by Dharmapala.[1] Well before Dharmapala came to Bodh Gaya in 1891, other Buddhists had ventured there to see the site and attempt to restore or rebuild the holy temple. Soon after the Muslims laid waste to the temple around 1200 C.E., a Tibetan monk named Dharmasvamin came and found it in ruins. Through the years other Buddhist pilgrims—Nepalese, Chinese, Burmese—apparently visited the temple; we know of them through inscriptions and coins found at the site. In the fifteenth century, the Burmese sent a mission to repair the temple and its gardens, but they were thwarted in their attempts by the resident Shaivite priests. Again, they came, in the nineteenth century and were able to do some restoration on the temple. Sadly, in the process of restoring the site, they destroyed much of the archaeological value.[2]

Part of the difficulty of the Bodh Gaya struggle lay in the Brahman practice of subsuming Buddhist iconography and claiming it as theirs. For example, at the front gates of the Mahabodhi complex, there are shrines said by local Hindus to contain images of the five Pandavas, the heroes of the Indian epic, the *Mahabharata*. In fact, they are images of five Buddhist bodhisattvas.[3] Another difficulty lay in the absorption of the Buddha into the pantheon of Hindu Gods; that Hindus had centuries before appropriated the Buddha as the ninth incarnation of the God Vishnu is interesting. Hindus say that the Buddha was, in fact, an avatar "sent to destroy enemies of the Vaisnavas (followers of the God Vishnu) from within."[4] Scholars of Hinduism refer to such a tactic as "encompassment" whereby Hindus absorb distinct, even hostile traditions, into the larger Hindu system. In the process, the other gods are made subservient or often relegated to a lower position within the Hindu pantheon.

It is possible to imagine how the Buddhists coming to this Bodh Gaya must have felt, seeing the Buddhist statues dressed in Hindu clothes, with red scarves wrapped around the head, red powder smeared on the forehead and third eye. What the Buddhists did not understand, especially Dharmapala when he arrived, was that this practice of appropriation had been taking place for centuries and had become normalized for Hindu pilgrims coming to worship and to make offerings for their ancestors. Bodh Gaya was on the pilgrimage route for Hindus and was one of the most important sites on the entire Hindu pilgrimage circuit. Legends linked to the nearby town of Gaya identify it as the home of a demon named Gayasura whose wild yogic exercises threatened the balance of the universe. The gods asked Vishnu, to whom the demon was devoted, to stop him. Vishnu destroyed Gayasura by turning his body into the landscape of Gaya and thereby making it sacred. It became a place of honoring the ancestors and making offerings for their auspicious rebirth. The Gayawals, a sect of Brahmin priests, became the guardians there, claiming the land as sacred, and charged the pilgrims a fee to perform rituals and make offerings. Eventually, the Gayawals diminished in numbers, possibly because of plagues, and subsequently, offered little threat in the final struggle for Bodh Gaya.[5]

When Dharmapala came to Bodh Gaya, India was under the rule of the British and the people had been suffering from an imposition of Western Christian ideas, just as Sri Lankans and Hawaiians had been. Dharmapala thought he could reason with the British over the sacredness of Bodh Gaya and could convince them of the rightness of the Buddhist claims. Perhaps too idealistic about the British sense of fairness, what he hoped for did not happen for a long time and for a number of reasons. First and most important, the British, who had been colonizing the subcontinent since the 1700s, were experiencing resistance from the Indian population. With the Indians tiring of their servitude, the British did not want to incite the Hindus at that point in history. Also, the Archaeological Survey of India, under the direction of Alexander Cunningham, had interests in the Ganges Plains and particularly in Bodh Gaya because of its antiquities. The more the ruins were tampered with, the less likely they would be able to offer up information about India's past and to fulfill the mission of the society. Cunningham had a real interest in Indian history and particularly its Buddhist sites and monuments and he was an empathetic surveyor. However, it was also a period of great pilfering of sculptures and other valuable artifacts that were being sent home to the museums in London; it seems that Cunningham profited by his own vast collection from Bodh Gaya.[6] This "tradition" continued long after Cunningham left.

Cunningham's work took place between 1864 and 1866, and, after he left, the Burmese King Mindon requested that he be allowed once more to restore the Mahabodhi Temple. There was no objection from the Hindu Mahanta and work began in 1874 with Burmese workmen reconstructing parts of the old temple. There are various interpretations concerning the quality of their work but, suffice it to say, the temple did not resemble the original structure when they finished. In 1878, the Burmese workmen returned to Burma. Two Burmese Buddhist monks remained behind in Bodh Gaya and stayed in the Shaivite monastery.

The Shaivite monastics claimed that they had been given permission by the government during the seventh century to build a *Math* or Hindu monastery and temple on the grounds of the Mahabodhi. The British had accepted the assertion without documentation and considered the Shaivites' claim legitimate.[7] Dharmapala, influenced by Sir Edwin Arnold's *Light of Asia,* asserted another claim. From his diary:

"The idea of restoring the Buddhist Jerusalem into Buddhist hands originated with Sir Edwin Arnold after having visited the sacred spot in 1886. It was he who gave me the impulse to visit the shrine, and since 1891 I have done all I could to make the Buddhists of all lands interested in the scheme of restoration."[8]

Dharmapala earnestly tried to reason with the Shaivites over the matter but to no avail. His efforts were thwarted at all turns for many long years.

Mary Foster may have visited the Bodh Gaya site but no tangible evidence for that assertion survives. She and Dharmapala discussed the ongoing machinations there and the need for assistance in supervising the reconstruction of the temple. They also discussed ways to convince the British authorities of the importance of Dharmapala and his associates having an ongoing presence there. In fact, Dharmapala spent seventeen years in Bodh Gaya without making very much headway in either of those efforts.[9]

Asked to speak at the Bodh Gaya celebration of Mary Foster, I contemplated all the years of Dharmapala's struggle to regain the temple. I noticed the current Shaivite Hindu Mahanta sitting in the front row, waiting to hear me. So much had transpired in those 108 years. Still some tension continues between Buddhists and Hindus but it is kindness that lies quietly under the surface of the amiable sharing of control of the magnificent temple.

The actual struggle for the Mahabodhi spanned sixty years and because it was the main reason for Dharmapala and Mary Foster to meet initially, it is helpful to understand what was gained and lost in that struggle. Mary Foster contributed more than a million rupees (approximately $10 million by today's account) over a period of forty years to the effort, and like Dharmapala, she never saw the resolution of the problem of the temple's Buddhist jurisdiction.

Dharmapala's initial inspiration for visiting Bodh Gaya was due to Edwin Arnold's interest but it became his own personal lifelong project and passion. Arnold did not anticipate the obstacles that Dharmapala encountered in his attempts to recover the temple. He claimed that "the whole thing could be managed through amicable arrangements, between the various concerned groups."[10] However, in a study on the Maha Bodhi Society in Bodh Gaya, author Alan Trevitick noted: "Neither Arnold nor Dharmapala understood the extent to which the temple was embedded in a system of longstanding local and regional relationships, at a concrete social level, and neither did they appreciate the extent to which the Buddha, and Buddhism, were encompassed, culturally and ideologically, by Hindu practices and ideas."[11]

Dharmapala was, at first, unclear about whom was in control of the temple when he arrived in January of 1891. The superintendent of the temple grounds, an employee of the government's Public Works Department, told him that "the temple is under the control of the government but the Mahanta has the right of the management thereof."[12] Then, in March of that same year and in response to Dharmapala's inquiry into the possibility of purchasing the land on which the Mahabodhi Temple stood, George Abraham Grierson, the British Tax Collector at that time, told Dharmapala that "the temple belongs to the Mahanta, not to the Government" and that the Mahanta was unwilling to discuss its sale as the temple was sacred to him and not up for sale. At that point, Dharmapala returned to Ceylon and formed the Maha Bodhi Society to pursue his dream of returning the sacred site in Buddhism to Buddhists.[13]

In July of 1891, a group of Sinhalese monks accompanied Dharmapala to Bodh Gaya and Dharmapala attempted to negotiate a land lease with the Mahanta. Word of the offer was relayed all the way to Viceroy Lansdowne, who agreed with the local government officials in Bengal that the leasing or selling of land in Bodh Gaya required "buying the Mahanta out, and with the goodwill of the Hindu community."[14]

Apparently, Dharmapala understood the Viceroy's declaration as an opening to a successful negotiation and, as a result, planned a Buddhist Festival at the Mahabodhi Temple. In writing, he referred to the event as an International Buddhist Conference although it was attended by only a handful of Buddhist pilgrims.[15] The Mahanta lodged a complaint about Dharmapala's action that was sent to the viceroy. Lansdowne sent Lieutenant Governor Elliott to investigate. Elliott's opinion was that the Mahanta should be allowed to hold onto the temple but the Tax Collector Grierson felt that the government "ought to treat it as a national monument, acquire it and not allow it to fall into private hands."[16] Nothing occurred at that point to indicate that the government would actually acquire the temple, but Dharmapala began a campaign through South Asia and Europe celebrating victory before it happened. He inspired many people and garnered wide support for his project while seemingly oblivious to the desires of the Hindus or the British government. He wrote editorials in his newly established *Mahabodhi Journal* championing his cause and continuously seeking financial and moral support.

Dharmapala and his Theosophical mentor, Henry Steele Olcott, traveled to Bodh Gaya and together approached the Mahanta in early 1893. Both assumed that, since Olcott was respected by Hindus in other parts of the country, the Mahanta might be more amenable to selling if he were involved. Such was not the case, and a new course of action was necessary. Dharmapala and Olcott inquired about purchasing land near the Mahabodhi Temple but that attempt was thwarted as well. They then engaged Edwin Arnold to use his influence with the viceroy, but again, to no avail.

Dharmapala left Bodh Gaya in 1893 because he was invited to attend the World Parliament of Religions in Chicago. On his return home from that momentous event, he met Mary Foster in Honolulu and that meeting gave the young Sri Lankan the confidence and the promise of financial support that he would need to energize his project in Bodh Gaya. After his auspicious meeting with Mary Foster, Dharmapala traveled to Japan where he was given a tenth- century statue of the Buddha that the donors wanted installed in the Mahabodhi Temple.

On February 25, 1895, Dharmapala and three Sinhalese monks carried that statue to the temple in Bodh Gaya and attempted to set it up in the upstairs altar room. There ensued a confrontation with the Mahanta's attendees and the statue was removed to the open courtyard downstairs. The police were finally brought in and the mattered presented to the local British magistrate who heard the various versions of the event. Dharmapala filed a legal petition with the magistrate. Word spread to the British viceroy, Lord Elgin, who then traveled to Bodh Gaya to investigate the situation. After visiting the Mahabodhi Temple, the viceroy was disturbed that the Buddhists were not being allowed to worship there. In the meantime, the statue that Dharmapala had brought was missing. It was quickly found and reinstalled in the courtyard by the Mahanta's men, but that deed alone had consequences in court.

During the court proceedings, it was established that Hindu worshipers did not enter the temple because it was considered a Buddhist shrine. It was shown, however, that the Buddha had been absorbed into the Hindu pantheon as an avatar of Vishnu. The case surrounded the Buddhists' right to worship in the temple and the assault on them by the Hindus. The assailants were found guilty, so the Mahanta appealed. In the appeal, the issue of proprietorship became the focus and, then, whether or not Dharmapala had committed an illegal act by "trespassing" onto the temple grounds to worship. It was determined that Dharmapala had the right to worship and those who had prevented him were found guilty. The Hindus once again appealed to the higher court in Calcutta. The Hindus won the appeal and Dharmapala was forced to remove the Buddhist statue to the Burmese rest house.

Despite his win, the Hindu Mahanta continued to fight against Dharmapala in as many ways as he could. He even tried to claim the Burmese rest house as his property despite the fact that Buddhist pilgrims had been staying there for decades and the rest house had originally been built for the king of Burma.

In 1903, George Nathaniel Curzon, perhaps the most famous of the British vice-roys, visited Bodh Gaya, in an attempt to understand fully the ongoing struggle between the Hindus and the Buddhists. Curzon was inclined to believe that the Buddhists had a right to worship there because it was their temple originally as well as the most sacred site for all Buddhists everywhere. He interviewed the Mahanta and came away with the conviction that the temple belonged to the Buddhists. He felt that Dharmapala had been provocative, annoying, and had caused the Mahanta to become proprietary and defensive. After all, the Mahanta argued, it had been seven hundred years since the temple had been destroyed and the Buddhists driven out. The Hindus had been in residence for the last three hundred years with very little Buddhist presence. The battles went on and on with successive collectors and other officers of the British Raj taking their own opinions on the matter into the legal and governing arenas. In 1903, a commission was established for the purpose of determining the management of the temple complex and the rights of both the Hindus and the Buddhists. Unfortunately, the commission failed to solve the various issues. Dharmapala and his supporters then turned to the legislative bodies for support. The discourse of mutuality emerged wherein that both Hindus and Buddhists had spiritual ties to Bodh Gaya and a new conversation of cooperation developed. At the India National Congress in 1925, Dharmapala asked that the Bodh Gaya issue be addressed. The proposal called for a "joint committee" to be established for shared governance of the temple by Buddhists and Hindus. The congress tabled the proposal and Dharmapala, ill with heart disease by then, left India for Switzerland, to rest in a sanitorium to regain his health. Mary Foster, concerned for his welfare, covered his expenses.

In 1928, Dharmapala returned to India but devoted his attention to the new London Mahabodhi Center and other developing projects. He was largely uninvolved in the final phases of negotiations over the Bodh Gaya temple. Eventually, he was ordained as a Buddhist monk in Sarnath and took the name Devamitta Dhammapala; there he lived until his death in 1933.

The Burmese delegation to the India National Congress continued the fight that Dharmapala left behind. They presented a much more cooperative plan for shared management. The Burmese contingent joined forces with the new leadership of the Maha Bodhi Society and presented a face of compromise and brotherhood. From 1935 to 1949, several bills and proposals were brought before the national legislative bodies. Finally a successful bill was initiated and passed at the provincial level that created a management committee, composed of three Buddhists, three Hindus, and the elected representative from the district. The bill passed in 1949 and the transfer ceremony finally took place in 1951. That agreement remains in place today despite the fact that Dharmapala would have been concerned to see continued Hindu influence on the committee. Today, it appears that the committee has some semblance of balance and cooperation and that they make fair decisions regarding the temple and its worshippers. Still, scandals and intrigue continue to emerge almost as easily as they disappear.

The struggle for the Mahabodhi Temple continued for over sixty years and Mary Foster supported Dharmapala in all of his efforts regarding it. Mary was ecumenical, open-minded, and pluralistic. Dharmapala's growing rigidity and intolerance toward the Hindus and their claims were counter to her own beliefs and, yet, she wholeheartedly supported his position. It seems that he had grown frustrated and had tried more "radical" means. If Mary recognized that Dharmapala was unreasonable on some points, she never revealed it in her writings to him. Perhaps she did not fully realize the ramifications of Dharmapala's actions and his methods. It is possible that she was blinded by her steadfast belief in his motives and intentions. We will never really know what she felt about the Bodh Gaya project but we do know that she was sad not to see its resolution. She wrote about the matter to Dharmapala toward the end of her life. In 1927, she expressed, "For all your hard work and effort, it is unfortunate to receive no positive outcome. Perhaps the time will come when there will a resolution that will be satisfactory to you and will have great benefit to Buddhists everywhere."[16] As for Dharmapala, surely, he was drained by his personal forty-year battle for the Mahabodhi Temple. Overwhelmed by his own impending death, he finally surrendered to the fact that he would not live to see its completion.

Returning to the celebration at the Mahabodhi honoring Mary Foster, I ultimately spoke of the parallels in her life with those of Dharmapala and made no mention of the struggle for Bodh Gaya and the Mahabodhi Temple. Rather, I told the audience about Mary Foster, about her struggles in her island home and her desire to relieve the suffering of people, both in Hawai'i and in Asia. I explained that she was an indigenous person, oppressed by outsiders who came to her land, just as the Muslims and the British had come to India and had destroyed what the people there had felt was sacred. I spoke about Mary Foster's first meeting with Anagarika Dharmapala, how she had been so taken with his sincerity and selfless desire. It was important to convey what an unusual woman Mary Foster was for her time, and, for that matter, probably for any time. I talked about the overthrow of her Hawaiian Queen and how distraught Mary Foster was as a result, and how Buddhism and the practice of Vipassana Meditation had helped her to cope and survive her own difficulties. Included were some passages from Dharmapala about Mary Foster in which he praised her character and generosity: "For the good of Buddhists, a lady from the distant island of Honolulu in the Pacific Ocean, has continuously sent help and assistance. We render Mrs. Foster our grateful thanks."[17] And again, "Mrs. Foster's generous benefactions amount to a great deal of money, but it is more than that. I have deemed her 'the queen of the empire of righteousness.'" He also told of George Mead, speaking at the London meeting of the Maha Bodhi Society, who said, "Mrs. Foster and Dharmapala had a romance of unparalleled generosity." When his own mother died, Dharmapala took to calling Mary Foster his "foster mother." Theirs was a deep spiritual friendship or *kalyana mitra* in Buddhist terms.

It seemed imperative to leave the audience at the Mahabodhi Temple with an understanding of the respect and friendship that Mary Foster and Dharmapala felt for each other and their impact on each other and in the world. The talk ended with a recitation of the Heart Sutra, one of Dharmapala's favorite texts. I looked over to the Mahanta and noticed he glimmer of a smile on his wizened face.

Chapter Nine

KAHANA VALLEY

A large part of Mary Foster's fortune endowed to her many charities, both Buddhist and Hawaiian, were connected to Kahana Valley on the Windward side of O'ahu. Mary Foster built a country home on Kahana Bay for weekend visits and family parties. A song was written for her called "Beautiful Kahana" by Mary J. Montano and Charles E. King.[1] Visiting merchant ships needed provisions and trade goods. Produce, pigs, and trees were loaded on to steamers like the *Matilda* and the *Mary E. Foster*, registered under the flag of the Interisland Steam Navigation Company.[2] Such vessels carried the load up around Kaena Point and down into Honolulu Harbor, a good day's journey that the Hawaiians had made for centuries. Thomas Foster, Mary's husband, through his interisland shipping recognized that Kahana Bay was hospitable to boats, and the Chinese and Hawaiian farmers in Kahana welcomed his transport of their goods to the city.

Thomas Foster first bought land in Kahana in 1888, seven shares that had belonged to King Kalākaua and he eventually accumulated twelve more shares before he died in 1889. His father-in-law, James Robinson, also accumulated land in Kahana, mostly through loans to farmers that they never repaid or traded. The biggest investor in Kahana, however, was Mary Foster, herself. By the time she died in 1930, Mary Foster owned 99 percent of Kahana Valley's 5,015 acres. The story of those purchases and the larger controversy around landownership is part of Mary Foster's legacy. It began with the Mahele.

The Mahele

What has been called the "Great" Mahele was composed of several laws and a process that forever changed Hawai'i and Hawaiians. Mahele means "division" in the Hawaiian language and has larger meanings than its literal translation, referring specifically to a land division process that took place between 1846–1855 but had dire repercussions for Hawaiians that continue in the present.

Even before the Mahele laws, there were plans afoot to change the rights to land and tenancy. Bob Stauffer tells us that American-born "advisors" to the Hawaiian kingdom wrote acts and laws such as the Organic Acts of 1845 and 1846 that not only established three branches of government in Hawai'i, but also created a board of commissioners to investigate claims of individuals to ownership of landed property. The "advisors" eventually became the Land Commission and their work was the precursor of the Mahele laws and the irreparable damage they created.[3] The Mahele, which was followed by the infamous Mortgage Act of 1874, could be called the nails in the proverbial coffin with regard to land rights in Hawai'i.

It began with Kamehameha III. Toward the end of his reign (1825–1854), the traditional system of land use underwent dramatic changes. Guided by foreign advisors, the king divided lands that had formerly been held in common and administered by chiefs and their konohiki or overseers. The Mahele allocated 23 percent of land in the Islands to the king (later called crown lands), 40 percent was designated as konohiki lands to be divided among 245 chiefs, and 37 percent was declared government land that was to be awarded to commoners who worked the land as active tenants. The appointed Land Commission and Court of Claims administered the land division.[4]

Bob Stauffer's book, *Kahana: How the Land Was Lost* (2004), is the most complete study of landownership and the Kahana Valley. In the introduction, he noted: "What the Great Mahele did was to create, for the first time, land titles to *kuleana*—homestead plots of the people—and to *ahupua'a*—land districts of the *ali'i*, the rulers".[5] Most people think that the kuleana lands were lost soon after the Mahele but, in fact, Stauffer wrote that "the lands remained unalienated (sold or lost) for a generation. The actual loss of the homestead lands did not occur until the passing of the Mortgage and Foreclosure Law in 1874 and most were not sold or appropriated until the late 1880s."[6]

The Kuleana Act of 1874 established fee simple ownership of land. What fee simple means is that you own both the land and the structure on that land. Historical land tenants were required to document their claims on specific parcels in order to gain permanent title. Once granted, a kuleana plot was entirely independent of the **traditional ahupua'a** in which it was situated and it could be sold to parties with no historical ties to the 'āina. What that meant was the land once cared for by distinct Hawaiian familial groups was lost to settlers and speculators.

Ahupua'a, the word describing a division of land capable of supporting a community, was traditionally part of a complex system of land division in pre-contact Hawai'i. Most ahupua'a ran from the mountains to the sea, and provided access to a full range of resources for the people to live. Traditionally, all land was controlled by the highest chief or king who held it in trust for the whole population. The king designated the supervisor of the land based on the chiefs' rank and standing.

Shaped by island geography, each ahupua'a followed the natural boundaries of the watershed. Each ahupua'a contained the resources that the human community needed, from fish and salt, to fertile land for farming taro or sweet potato, to koa and other trees growing in upslope areas. It was a holistic ecosystem with villagers from the coast trading fish for other foods or wood to build canoes and houses. Specialized knowledge and resources were also shared among ahupua'a.[7] There were kahuna lapa'au (medicinal herbalists), kumu hula (dance and chant teachers), and kahuna kalai wa'a (canoe carpenters) to name a few of the respected masters, who all gave their special skills to the community.

Although there was no private ownership of property, land tenure of the maka'ainana (commoners) was stable. Tenants paid weekly labor taxes, perhaps in the form of produce, fine mats, feather capes, wood and special taro, and annual taxes to the konohiki or local overseer who collected goods to support the chief and his court. The konohiki supervised communal labor within the ahupua'a, and also regulated land, water, and ocean use.

Stewardship of the land and its resources was formalized through the kapu (taboo) system. A kapu, administered and enforced by konohiki and kāhuna or priests, placed restrictions on fishing certain species during specific seasons, on gathering and replacing certain plants, and on many aspects of social interaction as well. In that way, the community maintained a balanced and sustainable lifestyle that paid attention to environmental needs.

A relationship with the environment, careful monitoring of the fishponds, the rotation of crops, and the kapu eventually forged unwritten laws that were shared and enforced by the chiefs' attention to the community. Through sharing resources and constantly working within the rhythms of the natural environment, Hawaiians enjoyed an abundant quality lifestyle with leisure time for recreation during the harvest season (makahiki).[8]

Given the fact that Hawaiians had thrived for millennia with their sustainable land system, it is no wonder that they balked at the intentions of the Mahele and the notion of privately owned property. Certainly, there was resistance but, in the hierarchical system of the chiefs and the ruling monarch, their voices were not heeded. One attempt at resistance was through the creation of the hui.

The Hawaiian Hui Movement

The Hawaiian Hui Movement started in the 1870s and continued until the 1920s. A hui is a kind of cooperative that was introduced by the Chinese. The hui, made up of Hawaiians, Chinese, and others, was established to buy and manage ahupuaʻa in an organized and well-thought out way to modernize a traditional system of living on the land together. According to Stauffer, the hui gave each family use rights to a homestead, and an undivided use right to the remainder of the land division and its offshore fishery.[9] In the end, the Hui Movement eventually died out because "shares" in the hui could be sold, and the capitalistic developments on the surrounding land were too big to contend with; but, for some critical time, it allowed for a kind of land management that was closer to the traditional ahupuaʻa system of the Native Hawaiians.

Kahana Valley (5,228.7 acres) was divided into thirds in the Mahele. The first third was divided among an aliʻi, Annie Keohokalole (mother of David

Kalākaua and Lili'uokalani) and thirty-seven families; she took the undeveloped lands and did not reside in the valley. The families received what were called kuleana homestead lands. The second third was taken by King Kamehameha III (Kauikeoauli) and the Royal Family; most of their land was mortgaged and eventually sold.[10] The last third was held by the government and was sold to investors and speculators by 1860. Western haole speculators such as Castle, Wilcox, and McCandless were the beneficiaries of those lands. Those holdings were eventually consolidated, but not without strong resistance from Mary Foster. By 1920, she owned 99 percent of the land in Kahana Valley.

In researching Mary's life in Hawai'i, I located thirty-seven legal-size boxes, each holding hundreds of pages of the conveyances and transactions having to do with Kahana in the Foster Collection at the State Archives. Mary Foster began buying land in Kahana in 1890, some say for investment, profit, and extending her land wealth, but given her many years of working for social justice for Hawaiians, her intentions were surely otherwise. Stauffer noted that Mary never used non-judicial mortgage foreclosure against a Hawaiian kuleana and that she worked to keep Native Hawaiians on their land.[11] She forgave loans and lent money to people who were in trouble with other lenders. She bought leases that were about to be foreclosed. She noted in her financial papers that it was essential to her to protect the kuleana families. She instructed her manager to work with care for those families.[12]

When E.H. Wodehouse married Mary Foster's niece Mary Iwalani Ward, he became Mary Foster's financial advisor and manager of her vast holdings. Her niece Mary, called May by the family, was the youngest daughter of Victoria, Mary's sister, and Curtis Perry Ward. In Mary Foster's papers and in her will, it appears as if May was not only Mary Foster's namesake but her favorite niece as well. Wodehouse was Mary's closest and most trusted business consultant. He encouraged Mary Foster to extend her inherited land holdings and buy properties in Kahana. She had already amassed large tracts of land, both in her own neighborhood of Nu'uanu and on the neighbor islands. Mary may have been conflicted about buying in Kahana because she had witnessed the dire consequences of the Mahele for her people. Because of a lack of understanding of the notion of private property among the Hawaiian people, she could see the devastating effects of mishandled land deals by unscrupulous speculators. Despite her charitable concern for the people and the mistreatment of their land, Mary had critics and foes.

The Kaneohe Ranch Company Lawsuit

Resulting from the Mahele, the Castle family, owners of the Kaneohe Ranch, raised cattle on most of what is now Kailua and Kāne'ohe. Emboldened, they decided to expand to Kahana. The ranch vigorously pursued and eventually acquired eighteen Hui shares and leased one additional share in 1879.[13] Why the ranch was investing in Kahana when the return on their investment was lower than elsewhere on the island is of great interest to our story.[14] The farmers in the lowlands of Kahana were not interested in the upcountry areas and so, when the ranch approached the Hui in 1897, they were easily given approval to lease all the upcountry lands for $1 million a year. They immediately started burning off all the indigenous trees and ground cover to prepare the land for cow pastures. When Mary Foster and Wodehouse learned of the destruction of the native trees and underbrush, they were distraught. Mary Foster began a fierce legal battle that lasted from 1899 to 1901, when she finally purchased the Kaneohe Ranch's interest including their leases in the Hui shares; at that point, she had the controlling interest in Kahana.[15] Mary Foster and those supporting her took a two-pronged approach to fighting Castle. First, she pursued the legal avenue and, secondly, she increased her power and presence within the Hui by purchasing more shares and, thus, acquired more voting rights. The Kaneohe Ranch responded by buying more shares and by pouring resources into the legal battle. Mary Foster's lawyers eventually wore down the ranch and an out-of-court settlement was finally reached. The Hui lease to the upcountry lands was cancelled and Mary Foster paid the ranch for its investment. By 1903, the large number of shares that she received from the ranch as well as earlier acquisitions gave Mrs. Foster the controlling interest in the entire Kahana ahupua'a. Mary Foster must have felt great satisfaction in defeating Castle, the owner of Kaneohe Ranch, and his attorney, Lorrin Thurston, in that both men had played major roles in the overthrow of Queen Liliʻuokalani and the destruction of the monarchy. That legal win was a small victory for her people.

In retaliation, Castle and Thurston struck again. Castle owned a small railroad called the Koolau Railway Company that ran from Kahuku to Honolulu Harbor. Castle was somehow able to manipulate government powers of eminent domain to gain ownership of the right-of-way to traverse Kahana from west to east and to continue down the coast to Kāneʻohe. Of course, Mary Foster protested vehemently and the railway line never came farther than Kahana. However, the Territorial Government, in retaliation to Mary Foster and her Royalist position, took a part of her land for use in improving the old government coastal trail through the valley. That trail eventually became Kamehameha Highway. In exchange, Mrs. Foster was given part of the government's only remaining Kahana landholding.

McCandless Water Case

More difficulties occurred for Mary Foster in another case in Kahana over water, this time with a man named Lincoln McCandless. Lincoln McCandless and his brothers arrived in the Islands in the early 1900s. They had been artesian-well drillers and they saw an opportunity to get rich with the development of the sugar plantations in the ʻEwa plain. McCandless believed that fresh water existed inside the Koʻolau mountain range that was the source of the streams along the Koʻolau coast. According to the land control agreements of the past, control of the underground water belonged to the owner of the land above it. McCandless bought up land in the back of Waiāhole, Waikāne, and Kahana. He then set about digging thirty-two miles of tunnels within the mountain range, collecting upland spring water in pipes underground, and delivering it to the Amfac-owned Oahu Sugar Company near Wahiawa. The maneuvering of McCandless to buy shares in Kahana only energized Foster and Wodehouse when they discovered what he was doing. The tunnels were constructed between 1913–1916. Upon completion, Mary Foster initiated a suit against McCandless because he was, in effect, siphoning the water that should have flowed to her land and the entire land of the lower valley. The court cases lasted until 1919 when Mary Foster settled out of court with McCandless and his agent, James Armstrong. The two drillers saw a large profit because the court sided with them. Mary Foster's heirs, however, were able to finally obtain the water rights in the 1960s when the McCandless water lease expired. McCandless and Armstrong were motivated solely by personal greed and cost Mary Foster large sums of money. What was important was that Mary prevented the draining of Waiāhole, Waikāne, and Kahana valleys of their precious water resources.

By 1920, Mary Foster held ninety-seven percent of the land in Kahana and, by the time of her death in 1930, she held all but six parcels in the valley, less than one percent.[16] In an amazing Legislative Research Bureau report on Kahana, attorney and author Susan Jaworowski wrote: "From the standpoint of preserving the Hawaiian rural lifestyle, it is a pity that the kuleana shares were made alienable and eventually lost by the maka'ainana whose families had lived there time out of mind. However, if the ahupua'a had to be lost, losing it to an owner like part-Hawaiian Mary Foster, who wanted to preserve its natural state and fought burning the forests for pasture, was the best of the possible options. The Hawaiian families of Kahana, as well as the members of the different ethnic groups who had moved to Kahana, remained on the land on month-to-month tenancies because of Mary Foster. Foster continued to lease much of the lands she acquired, and to the lo'i of the Hawaiians and the crops of the Chinese rice planters were gradually added the crops of the Japanese sugar cane farmers."[17]

After Mary Foster's Death

When Mary Foster died, Kahana passed to her estate and was held in trust for her heirs. During World War II, the U.S. military moved the Japanese residents out and began to use the valley to practice jungle warfare. After the war, several people became interested in purchasing Kahana, including the heiress Doris Duke who wanted to use the bay for boat races.[18] The Legislature contacted the descendants of Mary Foster as well as private foundations with a variety of ideas for how to develop Kahana. In 1965, the heirs decided that they wanted to sell

Kahana and hired John J. Hulten, a land appraiser, to assess the value of the land. Hulten was also, as it turns out, a State Senator who presented a remarkable report on Kahana to the Department of Land and Natural Resources. In it, he recommended that the State purchase the valley and develop it into a regional park that would attract more visitors than Waikīkī.[18]

In 1964, the land had a total tax assessed value of $2,328,664, yet, in the following year, Hulten submitted an assessment of more than $5 million for the same property. In 1965, Kahana was reclassified from agricultural to conservation land, which lowered the value; nevertheless, Hulten was able to push through the sale to the State for five million dollars. The Legislature had originally appropriated one million dollars for the first of five annual payments to the heirs, but they rejected the offer saying that the Legislature could not legally bind future legislatures to pay the remaining costs. Then, the State moved to condemn the land for park purposes and paid off the five million dollars in five annual installments to the family. The residents of Kahana were given month-to-month permits and were told that the State intended to relocate them outside of Kahana.[19]

For many years after, the State was not able to decide what to do with Kahana. There were at least forty-nine different studies done by the Department of Land and Natural Resources. In 1970, a report was submitted by Tongg & Associates that called for creating boat marinas, three lakes, and a dam with a waterfall. The proposal included an option to charge visitors an admission for future development. The residents in the valley were outraged. They formed a group called Hui o Kahana (later renamed Hui o Kanani o Kahana) to protest the development. A Task Force was established by the State to study the situation and especially to devise a plan for the residents to continue living in the state park. Certainly, Foster would have found the situation heartbreaking. She had struggled against abuses to the beautiful valley and for protection of the residents there for so many years.

After a time, the Task Force recommended the concept of a "living park" and Governor John Burns forwarded the idea to the Department of Land and Natural

Resources. The State Department of Education offered a plan to make Kahana a "resource for student learning." Queen Liliʻuokalani Children's Center issued a report on behalf of the residents of Kahana that asserted, "Kahana is a place where Hawaiian, Filipino, Chinese, Samoan and other families have meshed together to form a distinctly observable lifestyle within which some of the skills, knowledge, and practices of the old culture are present. It is this lifestyle that the residents wish to retain." The Queen Liliʻuokalani Children's Center report noted that the State was the source of some of the conflict with the residents in that it had created great uncertainty about what was required of the residents and if they would be allowed to remain in Kahana.

The State ordered more studies and, in 1974, an architect named Hitoshi Mogi presented a plan called The Kahana Valley State Park. In it, among other things, he criticized the Queen Liliʻuokalani Children's Center report and distorted its findings, by stating that there was no cohesion among the residents and little involvement with each other or the land. In fact, the Queen Liliʻuokalani Children's Center report concluded that a real community spirit did exist that was centered on the knowledge and skills of the old culture. Mogi disagreed largely because his focus was on creating a tourist destination and he was not the least bit concerned with the community at all. Mogi's plan, fortunately, was eventually rejected.

The Kahana residents created plans of their own that were more culturally acceptable to them, and presented them to the State. Some of the ideas in the reports were accepted but the State continued to order more studies. In 1978, the State involved Mogi again and asked him to do an Environmental Impact Statement. Mogi again proposed an amusement park. He suggested that the residents should provide most of the physical development of the park as well as to develop cultural programs, give services for park operations, and serve as cultural demonstrators and teachers, all with aloha.[20]

The Environmental Impact Statement was publicly criticized, especially by the residents of Kahana who subsequently drafted a "People's Plan" and presented it to the Department of Land and Natural Resources. The People's Plan was modest, calling for "restored trails, irrigation systems, taro loʻi, restored fishponds, renovated houses, and a canoe hale."[21]

The report was rejected by the Board of Land and Natural Resources without reason.

Finally, in 1993, the State's leases were signed with the Kahana residents. Three years later, in 1996, the highly interpretive cultural stipulation that resident families must donate their cultural skills was addressed. A new advisory committee was set up and the committee recommended revisiting the development of a master plan for the valley. The committee met intermittently and made little progress toward resolution on the issues that plagued Kahana.

By 2001, most of the residents had built their homes on their allotted plots and had accepted the sixty-five-year leases and were donating the State-mandated twenty-five hours of cultural service. There developed at least three different groups among the Kahana residents, each having an individual viewpoint on the future of Kahana. One group favored working with the State to develop a Living Cultural Park, one group favored a plan that was more holistic and sustainable and involved more traditional ideas and processes. The last group opted not to cooperate with the State and to wait for more options. The three groups argued among themselves and never found common ground.

As of 2016, there was still no Master Plan for Kahana. Work on a new plan was revived five years ago. Since then, several new versions of the plan have been written, presented, and rejected. A planning class from the University of Hawaiʻi at Mānoa's Department of Urban and Regional Planning worked on consolidating all the various plans. The class came up with three possible, distinct plans, but none of those were accepted as yet. It has been suggested that Kahana should be managed by a nonprofit entity rather than by the State, but that proposal has gone nowhere. The frustration of the residents and the State over the writing of and accepting of a new plan is palpable.

One thing is certain. Mary Foster would have worked tirelessly for a plan that involved the residents and descendants of Kahana; that plan would have been sensitive to Hawaiian culture and lifestyle and would have respected the various ethnic values that are now a part of Kahana. Mary would not be surprised by the State's way of dealing with Kahana, nor by the contentiousness of some of the residents. Certainly, if she were still living, she would be actively participating and offering her ideas for a positive plan for Kahana Valley.

Chapter Ten

COLOMBO

In Sri Lanka in 1999, while working on my Fulbright research on Dharmapala, I was introduced to Mala Weerasekera, Dharmapala's grandniece. A beautiful woman in her mid-60s, Mala was the owner of Don Carolis Fine Furniture Makers. The furniture showroom was the same one that Dharmapala's father had built into one of the finest establishments in Colombo. Mala inherited the company when her father, Neil, passed away. Neil was the eldest child of Dharmapala's brother Edmund.

Mala and I met regularly and she regaled me with personal stories from the Anagarika's life, family feuds, and happy relations. I was struck by her openness and her ability to recount the family history in such detail. She remembered hearing about how her granduncle helped to revive Buddhism in Sri Lanka and what an eccentric and extraordinary man he was. I asked her to tell me more about the family relations and their genealogy and she gave me a thumbnail sketch of Dharmapala's family. Dharmapala was born Don David Hewavitharana on September 17, 1864, in Colombo and died on April 29, 1933, at the Mulagandhakuti Temple in Sarnath, India. He had three brothers and a sister and each of them had a place in Sri Lankan history for very different reasons. Dharmapala's younger brother, Edmund, born six years after Dharmapala in June 1870, was a political activist who was imprisoned for his role in the 1915 Riots in Colombo and died while in prison awaiting a pardon.[1] Edmund had five children, Neil, Raja, Daya, Sumana, and Devi. Mala was the child of Neil, Edmund's oldest son. Dharmapala was very close to two nephews, Neil and Raja; he took Raja with him when he visited the United States and Europe. Another of Dharmapala's brothers, Charles Alwis Hewavitharana, was his liaison in Sri Lanka when he was living in Calcutta under house arrest after the 1915 riots.[2]

Mala explained that her granduncle was revered and respected by his siblings, but they also found him a bit overbearing. She confided that he was more radical than any of the others except maybe Edmund. I thought about the conversations between Dharmapala and Edmund— particularly about the political situation in Sri Lanka in the early 1900s. Dharmapala was in Calcutta at the time of the 1915 riots, a watershed event in Sri Lanka's history, but he was arrested and detained in Calcutta by the British police for six years for inciting his brothers and others to revolt in Sri Lanka.[3]

His brother Simon Alexander Hewavitharana was the quiet one; he worked in civil service for most of his life. His youngest brother, Charles Alwis Hewawitharana, the one most influenced by his elder brother, assisted him in many activities and actions throughout their lives together. Dharmapala had a sister who was born when Dharmapala was fifteen and died when he was seventeen; her death had an extraordinary effect on him. He never again wanted to see a woman suffer as his mother had on the death of the two-year-old girl. He vowed not to engage in a relationship wherein a woman would suffer. He never married and, as far as Mala knew, he never even had a romantic relation-ship when growing up. His surviving sister, Dona Engeltina Hewavitharana, was always treasured by Dharmapala and he endeavored to protect and support her even after her marriage to Jacob Moonasinghe. Together, Dona and Jacob opened a Textile Training School in Matara near the family ancestral home. Dharmapala was generous with her as he was with all of his siblings. He took them on trips abroad, included them in his life and kept in close communica-tion with them even when he traveled and lived abroad.

Of the many interesting things that Mala related, was an especially striking one about Dharmapala asking his father for permission to leave the family and embark on his "anagarika" journey. His father reluctantly gave him his blessing, but it was not until many years later that Don Carolis really saw the importance of Dharmapala's life and work. He supported his son through all his years of searching, but he only realized when Dharmapala came back from the World's Parliament in 1893 the true significance of his son's life and activities. He came to understand the role Dharmapala was playing in the spiritual future of the Sri Lankan people and the importance of his struggle in Bodh Gaya.

After Dharmapala met Foster in 1893, his activities in Bodh Gaya accelerated and so did his other work with the dharma. Her generosity supported many of his projects to the point where many of them remain operable and relevant to people today. Mary Foster contributed not only money for those endeavors, but she offered other kinds of support as well. Dharmapala relied on her wisdom and her business acumen and consulted with her on many of his ideas and plans. They, together, impacted the health of the people in Sri Lanka by establishing the Foster-Robinson Free Ayurvedic Hospital. They upgraded the education of the Sinhalese monks and nuns by creating a school in Kandy that was later named the Foster Seminary. They assisted in relieving the plight of abandoned and orphaned children by opening the Foster Home, an orphanage and halfway house for abandoned children in Colombo.

In his own way of honoring Mary, Dharmapala championed the naming of a street after her. Foster Lane sits in the Pettah area in Colombo. Walking down that lane and looking up at the building that once housed the Foster-Robinson Hospital, it is easy to imagine the early 1900s and the hustle and bustle of the city. The Ayurvedic Hospital, built in 1914, sat on that small lane until 1969 when land was given to the Maha Bodhi Society to rebuild the hospital in a more spacious and natural environment. My research necessitated a visit to that hospital to learn more about Mary Foster's place and importance there and in Sri Lanka.

The grounds of the small hospital were spacious with trees and flowers everywhere: frangipani, coconut palms, and bougainvillea. It was surprisingly lush and inviting, especially in sharp contrast to the usual stark and sterile medical institutions in Sri Lanka, such as Colombo General Hospital. I was greeted at the garden gate by a small old man with twinkling eyes in a stern face. Herby Seneviratne was an 83-year-old ex-major in the Sri Lankan army. The last thirty years of his life had been dedicated to the hospital and to keeping Mary Foster's name and legacy alive. He was passionate about the work at the free hospital and conveyed his wish to contact the Robinson's to assure the family of its continued existence. He related the story of a visit from one of the relatives some years before but he had forgotten the name of the descendant and had no contact information for her. When I asked him if he ever met Mrs. Foster, he replied that he had not had the pleasure. Nonetheless, he felt that he knew her and he wanted to honor her memory by acknowledging her gift to the Sri Lankan people. He gave me a letter that he had written to her family and asked me to deliver it when I returned to Hawai'i. I thought to myself, to whom should I deliver it and with what possible outcome? It was not possible to imagine anyone in the Robinson family who would want to contribute to a hospital on a small island in the Indian Ocean.

I wondered if Mary Foster had ever visited the Foster-Robinson Ayurvedic Hospital. Did she ever make it to Sri Lanka? Did she spend time reviewing the hospital or the orphanage, the Maha Bodhi Society, or the sacred sites of Buddhism? In search of evidence, I looked at the archival registers of the Galle Face Hotel, one of the oldest hotels in Colombo. The Galle Face Hotel, built in 1864, was a favorite place for royals such as Queen Elizabeth, the Duke of Edinburgh, Emperor Hirohito, and other luminaries such as Lord Mountbatten, Aga Khan, and John D. Rockefeller. Mary Foster's name did not appear anywhere in the historical register. It is possible she stayed with Dharmapala's family. In many of her letters to Dharmapala, she asks after his mother in such a familiar and caring way that it suggests a personal acquaintance.

I also inquired at the Thomas Lipton Estate in Haputale. Perhaps Mary Foster would have known Thomas Lipton because of his love of the sea and boating. He had been a part of the America's Cup and an enthusiast of sailing through-out his life. The manager of the Lipton Bungalow had a registry of guests, but Mary Foster's name did not appear there either.

Then I found a photograph, which I had taken at the Foster-Robinson Hospital that might show that Mary Foster traveled to Asia. It was of a framed portrait of Mary Foster, which hung on the wall at the entrance to the clinic. The glare from the entranceway made it difficult to get a clear picture and parts of the photo were obscured by reflected glass. I asked Herby Seneviratne how the portrait came to him and he could not remember, but it appears that it was taken in Asia.[2] It may be the only evidence that Mary traveled to India and/or Sri Lanka. I found no other information such as ships' manifests that would verify her travel, but it is known that she traveled widely so a trip to Asia did not seem unreasonable. The photo includes landscapes and balustrades that appear to be in South Asia. It is difficult to clearly decipher the details but that photo may be giving us additional information on Mary Foster's travels there.

Mary Foster's most important and enduring projects in South Asia were the development of the Maha Bodhi Society and the restoration of the temple to Buddhists. The Maha Bodhi Society, as we already know, was originally established in 1891 by Dharmapala, to support the rebuilding of the Mahabodhi Temple in Bodh Gaya. Dharmapala's vision of reviving Buddhism in South Asia demanded an entire infrastructure that included re-establishing the Sangha, re-educating the people about the Buddha and the Buddhist teachings, attending to the physical needs of people in order for them to engage in the dharma. There were health care issues, education issues, and basic living issues that were all overseen by the Maha Bodhi Society and Dharmapala. Mary Foster gave endlessly to each of the projects to support Dharmapala's good works. She would have wanted to visit the sacred sites and see the fruition of the projects. Yet, we find little extant evidence to suggest that she did.

Images of Mary Foster

It was interesting to discover during my research how Mary Foster was viewed by others. For example, when I was in Sri Lanka, I was invited to a talk by Dr. Kumari Jayawardene, a leading sociologist and feminist scholar in Sri Lanka. She had written a very compelling book called *The White Woman's Other Burden: Western Women and South Asia During British Rule.* It included a chapter about Mary Foster. Jayawardene claims that her intention in writing the book was to discuss various types of Western women with a "cause" who were linked to South Asia in the colonial period. She categorized them in telling ways: first, those who were intent on bringing Western ideas, education, religion, social reforms to the women of Asia; second, those were who rejected Christianity and Western values and were rediscovering Oriental religions and cultures. All of them, she claimed, had the "white woman's other burden," which was an attempt to liberate women in terms of a Western or Eastern ideal, and a vision of a better society.[3] Mary Foster was erroneously included in that second grouping. She was described in the section entitled: "Women Orientalists, Writers, and Funders" as "an American theosophist from Hawaii who, over a period of thirty years, financed Buddhist activities in India, Sri Lanka, and Europe."[4] No mention was made of her Native Hawaiian roots, or her extraordinary work and activities concerning social justice in her homeland. After her talk, I spoke with Dr. Jayawardene and she was shocked to learn about Mary Foster's background. Learning of Mary's heritage did shift her analysis, at least in terms of Mary Foster's place in this study. She was correct in her accounting of the relationship between Foster and Dharmapala, but not in the details and motivations of Mary Foster herself. Her primary source of information was Rhoda Hackler's *History of Foster Park and Garden (1986)*. What is surprising is that her Maha Bodhi Society contacts did not alert her to Mary Foster's native roots and her own experiences of oppression in the Hawaiian colonial experience.

The author did emphasize Mary Foster's generosity, particularly in her ongoing contributions to Dharmapala's seemingly endless projects. She wrote: "Anagarika Dharmapala's work for Buddhist revival through the Maha Bodhi societies and through his Buddhist organization in London were dependent on the generous funding he received from Mary Foster." She listed several contributions from Mary Foster to Dharmapala over many years, that she gleaned from Ananda Guruge's book *Return to Righteousness* and finally she opines about Mary Foster, "To the Buddhists of Sri Lanka she was certainly the white goddess of plenty."[5]

Dr. Jayawardene provides an unfortunate characterization that seems to sideline the remarkable work that Mary Foster did with Dharmapala. It also misses how Mary Foster struggled within her own island home. She neglected to address Mary's identity as a Native Hawaiian woman in a time of great oppression in Hawai'i and, instead, placed her within a context where she did not belong.

Another characterization of Mary Foster in Sri Lanka was revealed to me by Robert Aitken Roshi, a renowned Zen Master living in Honolulu. He told me that, in 1965, he had been asked by the East-West Center to review a folder of materials on Mary Foster for its Buddhist content. The materials had been collected by a cultural affairs officer at the American Embassy in Sri Lanka and were brought back from Colombo by John Hendrickson, the then vice chancellor at the Institute for Student Exchange at the East-West Center. When visiting Sri Lanka, Hendrickson had been approached by the young cultural affairs officer, Martin Carroll, who told him about notes that he had been gathering for some time on a remarkable lady from Honolulu named Mary Foster. Mr. Carroll suggested that the material would make an excellent thesis for a graduate student. The vice chancellor presented the notes to Dean Shunzo Sakamaki of the East-West Center. The vice chancellor also asked Aitken Roshi and Charles Hunter, a historian interested in Buddhism in Hawai'i during the period of Mary Foster's life, to read through the materials. Not long after, the vice chancellor received a somewhat cryptic note from Charles Hunter to Dean Sakamaki that contained the following assessment: "In regard to Mrs. Mary Foster and J.R. Hendrickson, if I were Hendrickson I'd quit while I was ahead. The family doesn't want the Honolulu side of this picture. Mrs. Foster was one of the Ward sisters of Old Plantation fame. Her adviser, John Waterhouse, her family (the Hustaces, etc.) were fit to be tied because of her financial activities and the story from this side would not win friends and influence people in India—if that is what Hendrickson has in mind."[6]

That short note contained so much incorrect information: Mary Foster was not a Ward sister but the aunt of those sisters, and her advisor was Ernest Wodehouse, not John Waterhouse. Furthermore, it was particularly interesting to read how some members of her family viewed her generous activities, if Hunter's words are factual. The material that Martin Carroll had collected was of great importance to Mary Foster's story. Reading through those papers, I discovered a treasure trove of information. There were financial reports that indicated that Mary Foster gave Dharmapala and the Maha Bodhi Society the equivalent today of nearly $10 million over forty years for their work. There were letters from Mary Foster to Dharmapala that revealed "her true voice." These were among the few personal letters that clearly showed the nature of their relationship and their mutual respect.

The fact that the story was silenced in 1965 and that, at least according to one person, the family "did not want the story told," left me wondering if any of it was true? One wonders what would have compelled the family to suppress her story, to erase her from public memory, and to claim that there was no information or family lore to share. One must speculate: was it that she was a woman out of her time, bold and independent, and willing to step out of conventional boundaries? Was it that she had different beliefs from the rest of her family and they could not understand or abide her interest in things so foreign? Were they upset that she gave so much of her wealth to a young Sri Lankan Buddhist monk for his social and spiritual endeavors? What might have caused them to regard her as a skeleton in need of closeting?

The papers from the cultural affairs officer provide yet another glimpse of her family. Charles Hunter's letter to Dean Sakamaki revealed not only the family's desire not to have her story told, it included an interesting postscript from his wife, Louise Hunter, a Buddhist scholar in her own right. It reads: "Shortly before she died, Mrs. Foster asked (the Buddhist priest) Rev. Ernest Hunt to preside at her funeral services. Unfortunately, she did not follow his advice by putting this request in writing—so, of course, when she passed on, the 'heathen priest' was ignored altogether and her family saw to it that she got the one thing she didn't want—a Christian burial."

We will never know the real reasons for the family's dismissal and silencing of the story of her life but one can only hope that some of the later descendants will see the worth of her life through this writing, and acknowledge her remarkable contributions to the family and to the world.

Chapter Eleven

HONOLULU

A Personal Reflection

As I gathered the pieces of Mary Foster's life and tried to understand her impact and legacy in Hawai'i and beyond, it was necessary to seek out her will and testament to learn what she had deemed important to pass on and to whom.

At the First Circuit Court downtown, I asked to see the files containing her Last Will and Testament. It was a will filled with codicils, changes, and challenges. I thought that she had had good relations with her siblings and I certainly did not expect to see what I did. In fact, I was shocked by the lawsuits brought by her descendants against her estate, accusing her of changing her will in the last year of her life because she was not thinking clearly or because she was under the influence of unscrupulous people. I did not remember seeing anything on her death certificate about dementia or what today we might call Alzheimer's. So, I went back to the State Archives that same day to review her death certificate. What I found was unnerving and very confusing. The archivist brought out the box with folders containing Mary Foster's personal papers including one with a death certificate. That certificate, however, belonged to her younger sister, Lucy McWayne. When I pointed that out to the Archivist, she was surprised and said: "That's odd, we don't collect for Lucy McWayne!"

How did Mary Foster's death certificate disappear from her archival materials? How and why was it replaced with that of Lucy McWayne? What happened to Mary Foster's certificate? I had seen it several years before. I had held it in my hands while sorting through the box of her personal papers. Who would have switched the two certificates? When I told Lucy McWayne's great grandson, Allen, he was extremely surprised. Allen is the McWayne family genealogist and one of few family members who had been helpful to me in my research. The fact that his great grandmother's death certificate was among Mary Foster's papers in the archives was news to him. One wonders how had someone made the mistake of mixing up the two sisters' death certificates or switching one for the other?

Later, I requested a copy of Mary's death certificate from the Hawai'i State Department of Health. It was unnerving to say the least. That death certificate had the word "Dementia" followed by a question mark that was typed on to her certificate, almost as an afterthought or an addition. Why and when did that occur and what, if any, meaning did it have?

Mary Foster did modify her will in the year before she died. In the modified version, she left more to her favorite charities and to certain members of her family than in the original will that was written four years before. The modified will was witnessed by two friends in San Francisco, so she probably prepared that new will while visiting there.

Some very interesting entries appear in the second will. In it, she increased support for the good work of many of her friends and siblings and left larger contributions to their projects. For example, she purchased a wing of the Queen's Hospital, providing beds for those Native Hawaiians who could not afford to pay. Her long friendship with Queen Emma, a woman she admired greatly, inspired her to support that very important endeavor. She financed much of the building of the Kapiolani Home that was the creation of her sister, Bathsheba. The Home later became the Kapiolani Hospital for Women and Children. She bought beds in that hospital as well, especially for Native Hawaiians who might not have been able to pay for them. She supported the Salvation Army and others who were offering services to her people. Her generosity was quite evident in the bequests, and she intended to have some of the contributions continue even after her death. She reduced some amounts to be given to her descendants, nephews and nieces of her siblings and they were disgruntled about that. Many of them retained lawyers to protest the changes. Perhaps Mary Foster felt that her money could do more good going to charities. Perhaps she was disappointed in the treatment of her in her old age by her relatives. Perhaps she felt they did not need the money as much as some of her other recipients.

Mary Foster spent most of the last five or so years of her life in San Francisco, returning to Honolulu only for the last five months of her life. In San Francisco, she stayed at various hotels and with the many friends she had made over the years there. Her sister Lucy owned a ranch outside the city where she visited and rested. It has been said that she and Thomas spent much of their time in San Francisco during the 1880s because they were saddened and overwrought about the situation at home. Mary Foster continued to visit San Francisco long after the death of her husband. She often went there before visiting Chicago, Seattle, and New York where her other sisters lived.

Mary Foster lived the last five months of her life at the home of her sister Victoria Ward. It is clear that she and Victoria maintained a close relationship throughout their lives and it is curious that Mary Foster was not mentioned in a book on the Wards. When I contacted the author, he said he had no information to share about Mary Foster.

Sitting in the Archives and reading through correspondence from those last years of her life, I learned that Mary Foster was well cared for by her sisters and friends. Of course her nephew, Ernest Wodehouse, took care of her vast estate and all her holdings. There are many letters in the Archives that are yellowed with age, brittle, and fragile. Some are originals and some are copies. One letter that is particularly poignant is from Mary Foster to Dharmapala. It was among the collection that had been carefully kept by the cultural affairs officer in Colombo. Dated May 21, 1923, Mary Foster wrote to Dharmapala urging him to take care of himself. She admonished him:

"My Dear Brother,
I note what you state in regard to self-denial on your part. The money sent you
is for you to use for your comfort as well as for the work you are accomplishing.
I am grateful to you for all you have done for me. Please grant me this one wish.

Searching for Mary Foster

Do take care of yourself and take enjoyment and make enjoyment by being with your mother more often. Live for your work, that is by taking good care of your health and give yourself more comforts… How often the thought comes to me how wonderful your work has grown. You must have given yourself very little rest to accomplish such good results. Words cannot express my gratitude, and how fortunate indeed it has been to me to have met a man so unselfish."[1]

EPILOGUE

Mary Foster was a visionary: a 19th century woman who was independent, intelligent, and fearless, a spiritual seeker whose work made a lasting impact on seemingly different worlds. She was determined to prevent social injustice in her own homeland as well as others. Her intellectual curiosity led her to seek out wisdom traditions and spiritual teachers, however far flung. She sought a spiritual path to deepen her own understanding and care for others. A woman ahead of her time, she was daring, outspoken, and willing to challenge entrenched powers causing havoc in Hawai`i. Her work at home and abroad contributed to the development of a more just, inclusive world.

It was a long journey looking for Foster, one that led me across the world, through temples, libraries, hospitals, and monasteries; to India, Sri Lanka, Chicago, and Honolulu. Along the way, her story became intertwined with mine. As a Buddhist, a seeker, and a single woman of mixed lineage—American, Northern European, New Zealand Maori—also trying to find my way in a tumultuous century, my own life story has been deeply infused with wonder and inspiration by hers.

GRATITUDE

There are always so many who create a story and who help to tell it. I feel immense gratitude for all the people who have contributed to the telling of this story, and encouraged me at every turn. I would be remiss if I did not acknowledge as many of them as I can. First, I want to thank Frank Karpiel, an old friend and roommate who shared his article on Mary Foster from the Hawai'i Historical Society. His research was the first definitive information that I received about Mary Foster, and I am indebted to him.

Kathy Harper, my dear friend who allowed me to live in her home for a month and helped to edit the book and make it more readable; Susan Killeen, who read through the entire manuscript and gave me more valuable suggestions; Kerstin Pilz, my dear friend in Australia who gave me refuge during my sabbatical so I could rest and write, and who later read through revisions of various chapters; Michael Schuster and Gayle Goodman who each read or heard parts of the story and shared their intelligent questions and ideas. Allan Seiden, who helped in so many ways: editing, helping me to rethink, asking good questions, and giving good suggestions.

Friends who lived with the writing of the book for twenty years include: Claudia Shay, my close friend who suffered vicariously as I struggled to write this book; Phil van Steenwyk, friend of my heart who patiently attended readings, asked some very interesting things, and still kept being friends with me; Rick and Annie Bernstein, dear ones who commune with me in a deeply spiritual way; Sally Klemm, confidante and friend who always has something good to say when I am struggling. So many more friends coaxed, cajoled, held my hands, prepared meals, and did so much to make this journey not only easier but pleasurable!

Stu Dawrs of *Hana Hou* magazine, my first editor of Mary Foster's story, in an article published by that magazine; Chris Pearce, a dear friend and the publisher of *Hana Hou*, the magazine that published my first article on Mary Foster; Craig Howes, who encouraged me to write this book about eighteen years ago when I was just discovering Mary Foster. His excitement for the project really spurred me on, even though I was not to finish the book until so many years after; Victoria Kneubuhl, who was also inspired by this story and along with Craig, helped me to present it in its early stages to the Distinguished Women of Hawai'i Conference; Karen Miyano, Paul Weissich, Corinne Chun Fujimoto, Heidi Bornhorst, and Grace Dixon—Foster Gardens friends who were interested and encouraging; the late Ruth Tabrah who wrote the Centennial for the Honpa Hongwanji Temple and really laid out the relationship of Mary Foster to the Japanese Buddhist community in Hawai'i; Allen McWayne, a member of Mary Foster's family, who shared with me so much, including showing me Mary Foster's Bible, which he now possesses; Liza Simon, who did so much research with and for me and became deeply involved in the story through that research; Amy Agbayani, my mentor and friend, who helped to fund the editing of the book, allowed me time to write, and supported me in so many ways over forty years; DeSoto Brown, who helped in the collection of photos at the Bishop Museum; TC Campbell, curator of the Abigail Kawananakoa collection who offered his insights and suggestions to find out more; Ron Williams, historian and expert on Hawaiian religions, including those related to the Theosophists and by extension, Mary Foster, who took the time to meet with me and share his knowledge. Dennis Keating took the photographs of Mary and Thomas Foster's burial site in Makiki Cemetery and I want to acknowledge him for offering those to me.

In Sri Lanka: Major Herbie Seneviratne, who kindly welcomed me and who kept Mary Foster's memory alive, performing a monthly *puja* to her at the hospital that she founded and he administered; Mala Weeresekera, Dharmapala's grandniece who filled in the Anagarika's story from the family's point of view; Saro Kadirgamar, my lovely host during my Fulbright year and sister-in-law to the great Foreign Minister Lakshman Kadirgamar; Kamal Kapadia, friend of my heart and co-conspirator in Sri Lankan adventures, and who vows to write something more about me and Mary Foster.

In India: Venerable Nyaneinda from the Burmese Vihar, whose mere presence inspired me; Robert and Diane Pryor who directed the Antioch Buddhist Studies

Program in Bodh Gaya and gave me the opportunity to first "find" Mary Foster in Sarnath; Venerable Molini Rai and Venerable Dhammavijaya, my dharma sisters who impacted my life more than they know; Ven. Sirisumedho, Chief of the Mahabodhi Temple in Bodh Gaya, and before that, the monk at Sarnath who originally told me to find out about Mary Foster; the Maha Bodhi Society that helps to keep the memory of Mary Foster and Dharmapala alive in India.

Ven. Lekshe Tsomo, who helped me to unwind my words from Frank's and helped to rework an article that appeared in her book *Against the Grain*; Ven. Ayya Vimala, who also has a great interest in Mary Foster; Joyce Spoehr, former educational director at Foster Gardens; and the Board of the Friends of Honolulu Botanical Gardens for their interest and their help all along the way.

So much gratitude goes to the Reverend Kevin Kuniyuki, Director of the Buddhist Studies Center in Honolulu, who gave his time and energy working with me, and suggested that the Buddhist Study Center might publish this book; Dexter and Faye Mar who allowed me to present parts of my text in different classes that I taught for their Dharma Light Series; Bishop Eric Matsumoto, who agreed to have the book published. I would like to also recognize Mai Frascarelli of the Bodhi Tree Meditation Center for her support, in many ways, in the publication of this book. She is a great supporter and a good and caring friend.

Finally, most importantly, my children, Kim and Justin, and their families—Lia, Justeija, West, Finn, and Bridgette, for always loving their crazy mom/grandma who traipsed all over the world and came home with fancy stories.

GLOSSARY

All items listed with their diacritical markings in the Glossary are taken from *Hawaiian Dictionary: Hawaiian English/English Hawaiian* by Mary Kawena Pukui and Samuel Elbert. Honolulu: University of Hawai'i Press, 1986 (6th edition).

'āina. n.	Land, earth.
ainoa. vt.	To eat freely, without observance of taboos.
ahupua'a. n.	Land division usually extending from the uplands to the sea.
ali'i. nvs.	Chief, chiefess, ruler, monarch, royal, regal, aristocrat.
'aumakua. nvt.	Family or personal gods, deified ancestors, protectors.
hale. nvt.	House, lodge, building, institution.
hānai. nvs.	Foster child, adopted child.
haole. nvs.	Foreigner, of foreign origin, as plants and animals.
heiau. n.	High place of worship, shrine, temple.
huna. n.	Hidden secret, hidden place, healing system.
hui. n.	Club, association, partnership, alliance.
kahili. nvt.	Feather standard, symbol of royalty.
kahuna. nvi.	Priest, expert in any profession (whether male or female), minister, doctor, magician, wizard.
kama'āina. nvi.	Native-born, host; acquainted, familiar.
kapa. n.	Cloth (tapa) made from wauke or mamaki bark.
kapu. nvs.	Prohibition, taboo, special privilege or exemption from ordinary kapu, sacredness, forbidden, holy, consecrated.
kekuanohe. n.	The back of a scorpion fish.

kīpuka. n.　　Variation or change of form; oasis; calm place

kōnane. nvi.　　Ancient game resembling checkers, played with pebbles placed in even lines on a stone or wood board.

konohiki. n.　　Headman of an ahupuaʻa land division under the chief.

Kuhina Nui. n.　　Powerful officer in the days of the monarchy; regent; prime minister.

kuleana. nvt.　　Right, privilege, responsibility, concern, authority.

loʻi. n.　　Irrigated terrace, especially for taro but also for rice.

makaʻāinana. n. the land.　　Commoner, populace, citizen, subject, people that attend

makahiki. n.　　Ancient festival beginning around October and lasting about four months, with sports and religious festivities and taboo on war. Harvest festival.

makai.　　Toward the sea.

māmaki. n.　　Small native trees with mulberry-like fruit that is valued for making tapa or kapa.

mauka.　　Toward the mountains.

pali. nvs.　　Cliff, precipice, steep hill or slope.

wauke: n.　　The paper mulberry favored for making kapa or tapa.

NOTES

Chapter One – Sarnath

1 There are varying dates for the Buddha's awakening. The most widely accepted date is 528 B.C.E. However, some scholars, including Richard Gombrich, have recently contended that he was enlightened around 400 B.C.E. The Buddha traveled from Bodh Gaya where he achieved enlightenment to Sarnath. Legend has it that his extraordinary vision allowed him to find the five ascetics with whom he lived for six years. They initially rejected him for his having left the group and then, later when they saw his illuminated presence, they approached him for his story. They became his first disciples and the first *Sangha*. What the Buddha transmitted in his first expression of his awakening is now recorded in The *Dharmacakrapartavana Sutra* (Skt) or *Dhammacakkappattavana Sutta* (Pali).

Chapter Two – Honolulu

1 Frank Hustace, *Victoria Ward and Her Family: Memories of Old Plantation.* (Honolulu: Victoria Ward Limited, 2000), 8.

2 Abraham Fornander, *An Account of the Polynesian People: Its Origins and Migrations, and the Ancient History of the Hawaiian People to the Times of Kamehameha I.* (London: Trubner & Company, 1878), 38. Fornander's book is held in great regard by scholars and others as authoritative and authentic in its rendering of historical moments from the origins to the time of King Kamehameha I. Fornander was a trained archaeologist and became the Circuit Judge of the Island of Maui. He married a Native Hawaiian woman and had one daughter. He lived over 30 years in Hawai'i.

3 Conversation with Margot Morgan on 11/24/2014.

4 Resources: San Francisco State Archives, Hawai'i State Archives, and Ancestry.com The Mr. Thompson that John Prever mentions in the letter is Prever's son-in-law, married to his second daughter, Kulamanu. They were known to James Robinson and lived near the Robinson's home. The letter is part of the archives of the Mark Robinson Estate.

5 King Kamehameha II (Liholiho) (c. 1797 – July 14, 1824) was the second king of the Kingdom of Hawai'i. His birth name was Liholiho and full name was Kalaninui kua Liholiho i ke kapu 'Iolani. He was born in 1797 in Hilo, on the island of Hawai'i, the eldest son of Kamehameha I and his

highest-ranking consort Queen Keōpuolani. He was groomed to be heir to the throne from age five. It was originally planned that he would be born at the Kūkaniloko birth site on the island of Oʻahu but the queen's sickness prevented travel. Queen Kaʻahumanu, another of Kamehameha's wife was made his regent (*Kuhina Nui*) when he ascended the throne. Liholiho officially inherited the throne upon Kamehameha I's death in May 1819. He was 23 years old. However, Queen Kaʻahumanu had no intention of giving him the actual leadership of the kingdom. When Liholiho sailed toward the shores of Kailua-Kona (the capital at the time), Kaʻahumanu greeted him wearing Kamehameha's royal red cape, and she announced to the people on shore and to the surprised Liholiho, "We two shall rule the land." Liholiho, young and inexperienced, had no other choice. Kaʻahumanu became the first Kuhina Nui (regent) of Hawaiʻi. Liholiho was forced to take on a ceremonial role; administrative power was to be vested in Kaʻahumanu. He took the title "King Kamehameha II," but preferred to be called ʻIolani, which means "heavenly (or royal) hawk." Kamehameha II is best remembered for the ʻAi Noa, the breaking of the ancient kapu (taboo) system of religious laws six months into his reign when he sat down with Kaʻahumanu and his mother Keopuolani and ate a meal together. What followed was the disbanding of the social status of the priest and the destruction of temples and images. Source: Kamakau, Samuel Manaikalani. *Ruling Chiefs of Hawaiʻi.* (Honolulu: Kamehameha Schools Press, 1961, 231). Also, unpublished manuscript by Allan Seiden on the Robinson Family, 2016.

[6] Ibid. Allan Seiden.

[7] Kakuhihewa was the 15th Aliʻi Aimoku of Oʻahu. He ruled as titular King or chief of the Hawaiian Island of Oʻahu. He was not only one of the great kings of Oʻahu, but was also celebrated throughout the eight islands for all the princely qualities that formed the ideal of a highborn chief in those days. The legends related to him are somewhat fuller or have been retained better than those of many of his contemporaries of successors. His very name is remembered in the poetic genealogy of Oʻahu. His birth date estimates are circa. 1540–1634. From: *Legends of Old Honolulu,* translated from Hawaiian by William Drake Westervelt, (Boston: George Ellis Press, 1915, 12 and 25).

[8] According to Peter T. Young's website, *Hoʻokuleana,* (totakeresponsibility. blogspot.com), Russians arrived in Hawaii in 1804 on ships associated with the Russian-American Fur Trading Company stationed at Sitka, Alaska, to obtain fruit, vegetables, and meat. During that timeframe, Hawaiʻi served

as an important provisioning site for traders, whalers and others crossing the Pacific. On O'ahu, in 1815, Kamehameha I granted Russian representatives permission to build a storehouse near Honolulu Harbor. But, instead, directed by the German adventurer Georg Schaffer (1779–1836), they began building a fort and raised the Russian flag. They built their blockhouse near the harbor, against the ancient heiau of Pākākā and close to the King's complex. There are reports that the Russians used stones from Pākākā Heiau in building their facility. As a side note, Pākākā was the site of Kaua'i King Kaumuali'i's negotiations for relinquishing his power to Kamehameha I. Instead of going to war, he pledged allegiance to Kamehameha a few years earlier in 1810. When Kamehameha discovered the Russians were building a fort rather than storehouses and had raised the Russian flag, he sent several chiefs, along with John Young (his advisor) to remove the Russians from O'ahu by force if necessary. The Russian personnel judiciously chose to sail for Kaua'i instead of risking bloodshed. On Kaua'i, they were given land by King Kaumuali'i; the Russian Fort Elizabeth was built there soon after. The partially built blockhouse in Honolulu was finished by Hawaiians, under the direction of John Young and mounted guns protected the fort. Its original purpose was to protect Honolulu by keeping out enemy or undesirable ships. But, it also functioned as a prison. By 1830, the fort had 40 guns mounted on the parapets all of various calibers (6, 8, 12, and probably a few 32 pounders.) Fort Kekuanohu literally means 'the back of the scorpion fish,' as in 'thorny back,' because of the rising guns on the walls. In 1838, 52 guns were reported. The fort protected Honolulu Harbor and also housed a number of administrative functions, including many years of service as Honolulu's police headquarters. The first courts of the Islands were held here until a new courthouse was built adjacent to the fort in 1853.

Barracks, officers' quarters, the Governor's House, prison cells, a guardhouse, and several powder magazines were inside the 340-by-300-foot-long, 12-foot-high and 20-foot-thick walls. The main entrance faced toward the mountains on Fort Street. The fort's massive 12-foot walls were torn apart and the fort dismantled in 1857 and used to fill the harbor to accommodate the expanding downtown area. Fort Street is one of the oldest streets in Honolulu and is named after the fort. Today, the site of the old fort is the open space called Walker Park, a small park at the corner of Queen and Fort streets fronting Ala Moana/Nimitz.

9 All of the children but Robert had long, successful lives. Robert died when he was a small child, most likely from one of the diseases that plagued the

Islands at the time. We will detail Mary's life in the body of the story but I wanted to give some background on the other Robinson children here:

Victoria, the second daughter, was born in 1846; she was the first of the children to be born at the Old Homestead soon after it was built. She was a very social person who enjoyed the balls and gala events in Honolulu. She married a Southern gentleman named Curtis Perry Ward and together they had seven daughters. They also had a son, Robinson Ward, who died in infancy. Victoria named her first daughter Mary Elizabeth in honor of her older sister but they affectionately called the child "Mellie." Victoria was perhaps the best known of the Robinson children. She had a fiery spirit that matched that of her Southern-born husband and she was often called the Belle of the Royal Set when she was a young woman. She married Curtis Ward when she was nineteen. All of the local newspapers called it one of the most elegant weddings that Honolulu had ever seen. King Kamehameha V and the entire royal court attended the ceremony, including Lydia Paki, the future Queen Lili'uokalani. The Royal Hawaiian Band entertained the guests at the reception at The Old Homestead. Over the years, Victoria and her husband amassed an enormous estate on 100 acres of land that reached from what is now Thomas Square to the ocean and from the Honolulu Club to McKinley High School. Under royal law at that time, their private property included the reef in front of the shoreline, and their fishing rights extended indefinitely out to sea. Ward Warehouse and Ward Centre occupy the area today. Three thousand feet of ocean frontage in that area still belongs to the Ward family.

Bathsheba, the third daughter, married Samuel Clesson Allen, a young American seaman who jumped ship in Honolulu and promptly asked James Robinson for a job. He worked for Mr. Robinson for some time and later became a partner in investments with Thomas R. Foster, the husband of Mary Elizabeth. Thomas Foster and Samuel Allen purchased schooners and sailing vessels that helped them to develop trade between the islands. The brothers-in-law together invested in many purchases but never became legal partners in business. Bathsheba was one of the most loved members of the Robinson family. Affectionately called "Aunt Batty," she always had big parties for the family at their home which was located in what is now the Richards Street YWCA. They had no children of their own but Aunt Batty was beloved by all of the children in the Robinson family. She is best remembered in Honolulu as the founder of the Kaiulani Home for the children of people who had been afflicted by Hansen's Disease. Sometimes called the separation sickness, and formally known as Leprosy, the afflicted were separated from their families and sent to the remote Kalaupapa peninsula on the island of Moloka'i. Some of them never saw their children again, and the Kaiulani Home cared for those children who were "orphaned" by the dreaded disease. Some of the relatives of the Hansen's Disease patients quite often would not allow the children of the patients to stay in their homes for fear of contracting the disease. Therefore, the Kaiulani Home was a blessing for those children with no other place to go.

Matilda, the fourth sister, married William Foster who was a saddle maker by trade and the nephew of Thomas Foster. They married in 1878 and William later worked with Thomas Foster in the inter-island shipping business. He had come to Hawai'i independently and stayed with his uncle until he could get settled in the islands. He met Matilda through her sister, Mary, and immediately fell in love with her. They had one child together.

Lucy Hannah, the eighth child and the youngest of the six daughters, was the last survivor of the James Robinson children. She passed away in 1943 at the age of 84. She married a young American medical student named Albert McWayne and they moved to New York City for him to complete his medical education. Later, they returned to Honolulu (in 1893) and he set up a medical practice on Alakea Street. They had three sons and one daughter. Their names were: Robinson Allen, Charles Andrew, Clarence Andrew, Clarence Scott, and Kulamanu Beatrice. When Dr. McWayne's health began to fail, the family moved to Kona on the Big Island and he founded McWayne Ranch where he ran cattle and raised coffee. He died in 1899 at age 46 and Lucy and the children moved back to Honolulu and lived with Aunt Batty and Uncle Sam Allen.

The Robinson family's love of the sea continued through this line of the family. McWayne's Marine Supply, a landmark for many years near Ward Warehouse was one of their thriving businesses. It was a continuation of the old Robinson Shipyard business founded in 1827.

Later, the Allen and Robinson business, successor to James Robinson & Company was absorbed by another company, Lewers and Cooke. Andrew McWayne, one of Lucy and Albert's children, kept certain interests that the old firm had handled. Andrew founded the McWayne Marine Supply with H.S. Gray and carried on the tradition of ship building, repair, and supply for which the family was so well known.

Mark Prever Robinson, the middle son, married Sophia Campbell, the daughter of Alexander James Campbell, a Scotsman who came to the Islands as a tailor and became a wealthy businessman in later years. Mark Robinson joined his brother-in-law, S.C. Allen (married to Bathsheba) in business and founded the firm of Allen and Robinson that dealt in supplies for sailing ships and steamers. They expanded the business into building materials of all types. They also owned and operated a fleet of coastal vessels that sailed from Honolulu to the Northwest and to San Francisco. In addition, they acquired an agency to sell coal in Hawai'i. They diversified and became very successful. The firm was eventually absorbed by Theo. H. Davies & Co. in 1930.

Mark Robinson became deeply involved in the political life of Honolulu during that time. He was first made the minister of foreign affairs in what was called the Wilcox cabinet, formed during the last year of Queen Lili'uokalani's reign. Then, after the overthrow, he became a member of the Council of State in 1896. Doing so was very controversial because the oligarchy was not seen as sympathetic to the Queen. Mark Robinson only stayed with that government for one year. He remained engaged in the political struggles of the time but did so from the sidelines rather than becoming fully involved again.

Annie Robinson, Mark's younger sister, was fondly called "Wattie" by the family. She was known as the "sweet one" in the Robinson family. She was said to have been kind and gentle and combined the best of both her Hawaiian and English ancestry. She married Albert Jaeger, a young German immigrant, in 1878. Jaeger had been trained as a forester but went to work in the firm of Allen & Robinson when he came to Honolulu. He managed their company for twenty years until he died. He is best remembered for his work in forestry and beautification of the city. In 1893, the government formed the Bureau of Agriculture and Forestry and Jaeger was made a commissioner. He personally chose and supervised the planting of the trees on Tantalus, thereby creating one of the most beautiful neighborhoods in Honolulu. The Jaegers had four children and lived out in the countryside, outside of Honolulu.

John Lawrence, the youngest child of James and Rebecca, married the Chiefess Caroline Kapu-ai-ana-hulu Johnson of Kona in 1884. John seemed to have the deepest connection to his Hawaiian roots and chose to build a house out in the plains of what is now Pearl City. He raised his family in the old Hawaiian way, speaking to his children in Hawaiian, and raising as much of his own food as was possible. His family perpetuated many of the arts of Hawai'i, including hula and the making of kapa.

[10] Clarice Taylor, *Tales of Old Hawai'i.* (first published as a series of articles by the Honolulu Star Bulletin in 1952), 18. This series was collected into book form and published by the Mark A. Robinson Trust in 1967.

W.D. Alexander , "The Oahu Charity School," *Hawaiian Historical Society Annual Reports* 11-19 (1908), 23. Reverend John Diell ,"The Oahu Charity School," *The Hawaiian Spectator*, Vol. I, 1838, 22-35.

Foster Family Genealogy, (Honolulu: Mark Robinson Estate), 226.

Thrum's Hawaiian Annual, Vol. LVI (Honolulu: Thrum and Oat), May, 1888, 19.

Personal Papers of Mary Foster, Hawai'i State Archives.

[11] Ibid.

[12] Genealogical Archives of the Foster Family, Nova Scotia.

[13] Personal Papers of Mary Foster, Hawai'i State Archives

[14] Conversation with Head Librarian at Kamehameha Schools, 11-12-14.

[15] Personal Diaries of Queen Lili'uokalani.

Chapter Three – Colombo

[1] Ananda Guruge, *Return to Righteousness: A collection of Speeches, Essays, and Letters of the Anagarika Dharmapala*, (Colombo: Ministry of Education and Cultural Affairs, 1965), 685.

[2] *Anagarika Dharmapala Personal Diaries*, Vol.II, now located in the collection of the National Archives of Sri Lanka, 42.

[3] Ibid.

[4] Guruge, 689.

[5] Ibid.

[6] Maha Sthavira Sangarakshita, *A Flame in Darkness*. (Calcutta, India: Tiratana Grantha Mala, 1980), 26.

[7] Dharmapala, Vol. XII, page 240.

[8] Ibid.

[9] Maha Sthavira Sangharaksita, *Anagarika Dharmapala: A Biographical Sketch*. (Kandy: Buddhist Publication Society, 1983), 45.

Chapter Four – Bodh Gaya

[1] Thapar, Romila. *Early India: From the Origins to AD 1300*. Berkeley: University of California Press, 2004. Page 184. Thapar offers another story – that of an anti-Buddhist fanatic cutting down the Bodhi Tree some centuries later.

[2] Ibid. 472.

[3] Dharmapala, *Diaries*, Vol. III, 45.

[4] Ibid. 50.

[5] Alan Trevithick's dissertation on the Mahabodhi Struggle and Tara Doyle's dissertation on Gaya and Bodh Gaya provide us with stunning histories of the most sacred site for Buddhist and Hindu practitioners and pilgrims who come throughout the year to the holy place. For more information, see: Tara Nancy Doyle. *Bodh Gaya: Journeys to the Diamond Throne and the Feet of Gayasur*. Ph.D. Thesis. Harvard University, Department of Religion, 1997; and Alan Trevithick, *A Jerusalem of the Buddhists in British India: 1874 - 1949*. Ph.D. Thesis: Harvard University, 1988.

Chapter Five – Chicago

[1] I had accompanied Dr. A.T. Ariyaratne to the event. He was one of the keynote speakers and had invited me to be there with him. I had worked with Ari for many years in his Sarvodaya Movement in Sri Lanka. Sarvodaya, which means "awakening for all" is a Buddhist-informed, community-based movement that has made a big difference in South Asia, and Ari has been recognized all over the world for his work. The history of the Movement is worth telling.

In 1958, Ari began taking his students out to villages in the southern part of the island where he had grown up to see how people there lived. When the group arrived in an outcaste village, even Ari was surprised. The people were visibly downtrodden and appeared to have given up hope. Ari asked the village chief what had happened. The chief explained that they had been paddy farmers but that they had no road to the big markets and had to rely on middlemen to take their rice to market. Over time, the middlemen had increased their own take of the profits and, as a result of their exorbitant fees, the villagers were starving to death. The villagers had asked the local government for help in building a road but had received no assistance.

Ari and the students organized a work camp, later called a "Shramadana" ("to give of one's own physical labor to benefit others"). They collected donations of equipment and materials as friends and families arrived to volunteer alongside the villagers at the camp. They were successful in building the road and much later Ari wrote of the experience: "we built the road and the road built us." All who had been a part were changed by that experience of giving for the good of others without thinking about benefit to themselves. They had helped to create a better life for that village and its people.

The news of that experience traveled throughout the country and soon, Ari was inundated with requests from struggling villages. He realized that the projects were not just a onetime charitable effort but that there was a deeper meaning to the work. He eventually gave up his position as a teacher and started organizing work camps throughout the country. Because Sri Lanka is 85 percent Buddhists, the notion of generosity and giving were part of a longstanding cultural tradition. They are basic tenets of the Buddhist philosophy and the Sinhalese people were accustomed to giving to those in need. Thus, it was fairly easy to engage people in volunteer efforts to help others. Once people heard the story of the selfless giving of Ari and his students and, because "making merit" is an important part of spiritual life in Sri Lanka, people began to sign up for the Shramadana work camps taking place all over the country.

What occurred to Ari at that point was that there was something more that could come out of the efforts. Deeply moved by Mahatma Gandhi and his movement, especially Gandhi's legacy in land reform and creating self-sufficient, self-sustaining communities, he traveled to India in 1960 to learn what he could about Gandhi's approach. Gandhi had felt that there must be a development of consciousness among the people about the imposition of Western ideas and development efforts and their impacts on the life of the people. Ari recognized that Sri Lankans were experiencing similar realizations, and realized that the village improvement that he was engaged in was a kind of community development that, if practiced consciously, could change the future of his country. With Western development models beginning to intrude on his small island nation, Ari came to see that he could introduce an alternative model for development that might even bypass the capitalistic moment and work to empower and enlighten his people. His idea was to introduce conscious development, coupled with an understanding of people's spiritual needs. He incorporated the concept of *arthadharma* – a Sanskrit word combining the words *artha* meaning "wealth," and *dharma* meaning "spiritual teachings" – as the necessary formula for sustainable development.

Some years later, E.F. Schumacher, the Harvard economist, wrote the book *Small Is Beautiful: Economics as if People Mattered,* after spending three years studying Ari's movement. For me in the early 1970's, *Small Is Beautiful* impressed me deeply. It was my first encounter with another way of living in the west. I was taken by his simple statement in the preface of the book: "Man is small and, therefore, small is beautiful." But Schumacher took me even deeper with these words: "Wisdom demands a new orientation of science and technology towards the organic, the gentle, the non-violent, the elegant and beautiful." His book became a guidebook for many in the early 70's, with its subtitle "Economics as if people mattered." It detailed how the concept of *arthadharma* – the balance of economic and spiritual development – was essential when considering development and a key element that was missing in Western development models. Schumacher had gleaned much of his thinking during his time with Ari and the Sarvodaya Movement and contributed to a whole generation of young Western people searching for a different way of thinking and acting.

The Sarvodaya movement was so successful that it has been recognized around the world. Ari was nominated for the Nobel Peace Prize twice and, over time, has received many other awards for his work and his innovative ideas. He was the recipient of the Ramon Magsaysay Award for Community Leadership in 1969, the Niwano Peace Prize in 1992, the Gandhi Peace Prize from the government of India in 1996, and other international honors for his work in peace making and village development. In 2006, he received the Acharya Sushil Kumar International Peace Award and, in 2007, he received the Sri Lankabhimanya, the highest national honor of Sri Lanka.

Ari held to the Gandhian principles of non-violence and self-sacrifice as he conceived his rural development model. The tenets of Buddhism also helped shape the Sarvodaya Movement in ways that forged a significant link between secular principles of development and Buddhist ideals of selfless-ness and compassion. As a devout Buddhist himself, he engaged monks and nuns in his development project and they worked side by side with the villagers. They participated in "family gatherings" where Sarvodaya work-ers would meet and discuss what they were doing and what needed to be done. The gatherings were joyful, full of music and laughter. There was also meditation and sharing of people's dreams, hopes and challenges. Ari also engaged the monks and nuns in mass community meditation gatherings where sometimes tens of thousands of people gathered meditate together.

When Ari received the Hubert H. Humphrey International Humanitarian Award in 1994, Dr. Patrick Mendis described his former mentor as the "Gandhi of Sri Lanka." Many have compared Ari to the great Mahatma although Ari himself would be embarrassed by the comparison.

[2] Hans Kung, the well-spoken Swiss theologian, scholar, and former Catholic priest, brought before the Parliament a Declaration entitled: "*Toward a Global Ethic: An Initial Declaration*" that sought a unified set of ethical behaviors across religions. He received tremendous support and thousands of signatures to his document. He intended to pursue acceptance of the document at the World Court in The Hague, the United Nations in New York and in other venues concerned with peace and ethics. He did, in fact, present the document as the "*Declaration Towards a Global Ethic*" to the U.N., which resulted in the U.N.'s project called A Dialogue Among Civilizations.

[3] Anagarika Dharmpala. *Personal Diaries,* Sri Lanka National Archives, Colombo, Sri Lanka, Vol. 6, 8.

[4] Richard Seager, *The World's Parliament of Religions.* (Bloomington and Indianapolis: Indiana University Press, 1995), xii.

[5] Ibid, xxiii.

[6] Other events took place in that year that also changed the course of world history. For example, Japan adopted the Gregorian calendar, changing how history was recorded there and how Japanese people were to understand their lives and times. Thomas Edison completed the world's first movie at Edison

studio in New Jersey, forever changing the imagination of people, young and old. New Zealand became the first country to grant all its women the right to vote and women voted in a national election there for the first time. Lizzie Borden was acquitted in the case of murder of her parents in New Bedford, MA; the first Ferris wheel premiered at Chicago's Columbian Exposition; the Excelsior diamond (blue-white 995 carats) was discovered; the first cultured pearl was obtained by Kokichi Mikimoto; Katharine Lee Bates wrote "America the Beautiful," in Colorado; Henry Perky and William Ford patented shredded wheat; France issued the first driving licenses which required a written and driving test and, at the same time, introduced motor vehicle registration; English author Beatrix Potter first told the story of Peter Rabbit in Britain; Shaku Soen became the first Zen teacher to visit the West; Cherokee Strip, Oklahoma opened a white settlement for homesteaders; Frank Duryea drove the first U.S.-made gas propelled vehicle and participated in the creation of the first auto built in the U.S. along with his brothers in Springfield, Ohio; Dr. Daniel Williams performed the first successful open heart surgery without anesthesia; Whitcomb Judson of Chicago patented a hookless fastening called a zipper; Nabisco Foods invented Cream of Wheat; RW Rueckheim invented Cracker Jacks; the State of Colorado introduced female suffrage. *(worldhistoryproject.org/1893)*

7   The Hui Aloha 'Āina (Hawaiian Patriotic League) was formed right after the overthrow to support the Queen and try to prevent annexation. The membership was comprised of 10,000 men and 12,000 women. The Hui Kālai 'āina (Hawaiian Political Association) was formed in 1889 to try to overthrow the Bayonet Constitution and claimed a membership of 17,000 Hawaiians and their supporters. (Noenoe Silva)

8   Noenoe K. Silva, "The 1897 Petitions Protesting Annexation." Unpublished paper, 1998, 11-27.

9   John Henry Barrows, *The World's Parliament of Religions: An Illustrated and Popular Story of the World's Parliament of Religions. Held in Chicago in Connection with the World's Columbian Exposition.* 2 vols. (Chicago: Parliament Publishing Co. 1893).

10   *The Daily Inter-Ocean*, September 20, 1893.

11   *St. Louis Observer*, September 21, 1893.

12   Seager, 45.

[13] Barrows, 455.

[14] Diaries of Anagarika Dharmapala, National Archives of Sri Lanka, volume 8, page 42.

[15] Ibid, 75.

Chapter Six – Honolulu
[1] Diaries, Vol. 8, 64.

[2] Ibid. 65.

[3] Ibid.

[4] Noenoe K. Silva, *Aloha Betrayed.* (Durham: Duke University Press, 2004), 124.

[5] Thomas Foster died unexpectedly in San Francisco in 1889. He was 59 years old. He and Mary Foster were there visiting friends and he died in the Occidental Hotel. I have often wondered: Did they keep rooms there? Did they have a house that was being built or possibly a country home in Santa Cruz that I have heard about recently? I heard they left Hawai'i because they were both so depressed and distraught over the current state of affairs in Hawai'i. It makes sense to me.

[6] Bouslog, Charles. "Doctor Auguste Jean Baptiste and Evelyn Oliver Marques." *The Hawaiian Journal of History*, volume 26 (1992), page 159.

[7] Ibid. Page 160.

[8] David Kalākaua, because of his undying love and respect for his Queen, Kapi'olani, and her selfless caring for the Hawaiian people, especially her establishment of Kapi'olani Women and Children's Hospital, and other projects, created the award and bestowed it on Hawai'i's residents who gave selflessly to the people of Hawai'i.

[9] Frank Karpiel, "Theosophy, Culture and Politics in Honolulu – 1890-1920." *The Hawaiian Journal of History,* Vol. 30 (1996), 176.

[10] Goldberg, Michelle. *The Goddess Pose: The Audacious Life of Indra Devi, the*

Woman Who Helped Bring Yoga to the West. New York: Vintage Books, 2016.

[11] Ibid. Page 22.

[12] Ibid. Page 23.

[13] Karpiel, page 177.

[14] Hawai'i State Archives. Mary Foster – Personal Papers.

[15] Countess Constance Wachtmeister (1838 – 1910) was born in Florence, Italy. Her father was French, her mother English. Research shows that after three years of marriage she moved to Stockholm where, in 1868, the count was appointed Minister of Foreign Affairs.[7][8] After the death of her husband in 1871, she still lived in Sweden for several years. In 1879 the countess began investigating Spiritism and in 1881 joined the London Lodge of the Theosophical Society. She met H.P. Blavatsky in London in 1884. She was an important partner for Blavatsky and essential support for the work of *The Secret Doctrine*. Some time after Blavatsky had come in 1885 at Wurzburg she was joined by the Wachtmeister, who "loyally and lovingly helped in the great work." In 1887 Wachtmeister organized the Theosophical Publishing Co. alongside Bertram Keightley, in order to publish Blavatsky's works. In 1888–1895 she was an editor of the *Theosophical Siftings*. She was secretary and treasurer of the Blavatsky Lodge in London. In 1890 she became a member of the Inner Group of Blavatsky Lodge. In 1893 Besant and Wachtmeister went to India. In 1894 she had a lecture in New York City on theosophical questions. In 1896 Wachtmeister toured the USA and Australia lecturing on Theosophy.

Wachtmeister did not leave many written texts, but her work, *Reminiscences of H. P. Blavatsky and the "Secret Doctrine,"* is a source for a study on the personality of Madame Blavatsky.

Wachtmeister stated that she spent a few months with Blavatsky. "I have shared her room and been with her morning, noon and night. I have had access to all her boxes and drawers, have read the letters which she received and those which she wrote." Wachtmeister, who became Blavatsky's "guardian angel, domestically speaking, during the years of the composition of *The Secret Doctrine* in Germany and Belgium, printed her account of a number of extraordinary occurrences of the period." In her *Reminiscences* Wachtmeister wrote in detail of the many facts coming under her observation, which pointed to extrinsic help in the Blavatsky's work. She wrote: "*The Secret Doctrine* will be indeed a great and grand work. I have had the privilege of watching its progress, of reading the manuscripts, and witnessing the occult way in which she derived her information."

Wachtmeister wrote, "When a printed copy of *The Secret Doctrine* was put into my hands, I was thankful to feel that all these hours of pain, toil and suffering had not been in vain, and that H.P.B. had been able to accomplish her task and give to the world this grand book, which, she told me, would have to wait quietly until the next century to be fully appreciated, and would only be studied by the few now." Axel R. Wachtmeister, *Memories*. (London: John Watkins Publishing, 1936), 123.

Chapter Seven – The Pure Land

1   During the preparations for the 125th Anniversary of the Hongpa Hongwanji Mission of Hawaii, I was invited by Bishop Eric Matsumoto's office to meet with Arthur Nakagawa, President of the temple. Eric said to me, "we are indebted to Mary Foster and want to acknowledge her during our anniversary celebrations this year. Can you help with some of the information you have?" I was so pleased to hear his acknowledgment and was reminded of my friend, Ruth Tabrah, who worked so hard on the 100th Anniversary book for the Hongwanji Temple entitled *A Grateful Past, A Promising Future*. Little did I see then that I was already on a path to knowing Mary Foster. Ruth was a dear friend and a devout follower of Shinran's teachings, the foundation of the Jōdō Shinshū School of Buddhism that the temple represents. I met Ruth in 1987 while she was working on the 100th Anniversary book and we became great friends through the Hawai'i Association of International Buddhists. She regaled me with stories of the temple and the history she was uncovering. I cannot recall if she ever told me anything specifically about Mary Foster at that time, but I do remember her excitement about her project and about the history of the temple and the school. I told Bishop Eric about the state of my research and how I had learned about the importance of the Honpa Hongwanji Buddhist Mission to Mary Foster. He asked me to recall some of the things I had uncovered about that aspect of Mary Foster's life and I shared the notes that I had researched for a presentation to the Hongpa Hongwanji Temple and for the book.

2   Soryu Kagahi was the first Hongwanji minister to come to Hawai'i in order to address the religious needs of Japanese immigrants. Upon arriving in Honolulu on March 2, 1889, the Reverend Kagahi rented a house and hung a sign, "The

Great Imperial Japan Hongwanji Denomination Hawaii Branch" and used it as a base for his religious activities. March 2 is now celebrated as Hawai'i Kyodan's "Kaikyo Kinen-bi" or "Hongwanji Day," the founding day of the mission.

3 He also traveled to Kaua'i, Maui, and Hawai'i Island to conduct religious services. He visited Hawai'i Island on two occasions and assisted the people in Hilo in founding the *Fūkyōjō,* the forerunner of the present Hilo Betsuin. (Hilo at that time had a larger Japanese population than did Honolulu.

In October 1889, the Reverend Kagahi returned to Japan to report on the Hawai'i situation and to urge establishment of Jodo Shinshu in Hawai'i. He also stressed the need for financial assistance to Hawai'i to carry forward those activities.

However, because authorities in Japan initially viewed the Japanese presence in Hawai'i as "transient," they did not see the need for a Hawaiian mission.

That changed in 1897 when the Japanese immigrants petitioned the Honpa Hongwanji headquarters in Japan and requested that Buddhist missionaries be sent to Hawai'i. They expressed the urgency and need for "community stability" – a stability achieved through religious institutions and the revival of cultural commonalities among the immigrants.

Leadership in Japan, once aware that the Japanese immigrant had become more than transient, responded enthusiastically, and more missions were established. The rise of Buddhism in a predominantly Christian environment was due, in part, to the deeper expression among the Japanese immigrants of their need for a sense of community. Several of the sugar plantations were sympathetic and supportive of the desire for temples and donated parcels of land near the immigrant camps. In 1898, Rev. Honi Satomi arrived as the first Bishop of Hongwanji, and property located off Fort Street at the end of Kukui, in the area called Fort Lane (just above Beretania Street and the Central Fire Station) was purchased for the first site of the temple.

4 *Commercial Pacific Advertiser*, November 27, 1900. Several articles in the Hawaiian language and English language newspapers also record Mary Foster's involvement in the Honpa Hongwanji during that period.

5 *Visuddhi Magga* or *The Path of Purification* was a fifth century C.E. text by the Buddhist Monk Buddhaghosa that gives guidelines to lay Buddhists

about how to lead a spiritually satisfying life.

6   Diary entries from Bishop Imamura appear in the Hongwanji 100th Anniversary publication entitled, *A Grateful Past, A Promising Future*, published by the Hongwanji Press, 1989. The primary writer and editor of the publication was Dr. Ruth Tabrah, a practicing member of the Hongwanji, and a well-known educator in Hawai'i.

7   *Mary Foster* File. Pacific Collection, Hamilton Library, University of Hawai'i, 1965.

8   *Issei* is a Japanese term for first generation Japanese who have migrated to foreign countries. The term literally means "first generation."

9   Dennis Ogawa, *Kodomo No Tame Ni*. (Honolulu: University of Hawai'i Press, 1978), 6.

10 The Satsuma Rebellion is one of Japan's most important historical events. The falling of Saigō Takamori, a famed Samurai and his *seppuku* or ritual suicide symbolizes the end of the Samurai era. It is a story that every Japanese child knows. Saigō Takamori's story was emblematic of the extreme changes that the country underwent with the opening of Japan to the West in 1868. After 200 years of isolation, with very little interference or interaction with the West, the Japanese leaders were eager to learn new technologies and to enter into global conversations and exchange. Some in the country, like the traditional Samurai, were threatened by the change and protested, sometimes to their death.

11 The ahupua'a was the traditional Hawaiian system of living and land management, based on moving from the mountains to the sea according to the seasons, and from the sea back up to the mountains, planting in the correct times and fishing in the correct times.

12 Ruth Tabrah, *A Grateful Past, A Promising Future: The First 100 Years of Honpa Hongwanji in Hawai'i*. (Honolulu: Honpa Hongwanji Centennial Committee, 1989), 17.

13 Ibid. 18.

14 Ibid. 19.

¹⁵ Henry Steele Olcott, co-founder of the Theosophical Society, figured in Mary Foster's life for many years. He had traveled to Sri Lanka in 1881 and met Dharmapala and sent him to India to be trained by Madame Blavatsky in the Ascended Masters study. Dharmapala, like Krishnamurti before him, eventually left the Theosophists to pursue his own spiritual path. He returned to Sri Lanka and began a deep study of Buddhist philosophy.

¹⁶ Tabrah, 24-25.

¹⁷ Ibid. 41.

¹⁸ Ibid. 42.

¹⁹ Ibid. 44.

²⁰ Ibid. 48.

²¹ The 442ⁿᵈ Regiment was composed almost entirely of Japanese Americans, despite the fact that many of their families were subject to internment. The Regiment, in fact, was the most decorated unit in U.S. military history. They were awarded eight Presidential Unit Citations and twenty-one of their members received the Medal of Honor.

The 100ᵗʰ Battalion was also composed mainly of Nisei Japanese, former members of the Hawai'i National Guard who eventually combined with the 442ⁿᵈ to create the 100ᵗʰ/442ⁿᵈ Regimental Combat Team under the 34ᵗʰ Division. An interesting aside, before the creation of the 442ⁿᵈ and the 100ᵗʰ Battalion, Japanese American ROTC students at the University of Hawai'i were told to report for military duty right after the bombing of Pearl Harbor. They were made guards in the Hawaiian Territorial Guard. When that came to the attention of officials in D.C., they were dismissed. The reason given to them was that "4-C enemy aliens were ineligible to serve in the military." The young men wrote a petition to the military governor at the time that read:

"We, the undersigned, were members of the Hawaiian Territorial Guard until its recent inactivation. We joined the Guard voluntarily with the hope that this was one way to serve our country in her time of need. Needless to say, we were deeply disappointed when we were told that our services in the Guard were no longer needed. Hawai'i is our home; the United States, our country. We know but one loyalty and that is to the Stars and Stripes. We wish to do our part as loyal Americans in every way possible and we hereby offer ourselves for whatever service you may see fit to use us."

In February 1942, the 169 ROTC students became a labor Battalion called the Varsity Victory Volunteers. In January 1943, the War Department made the announcement that an all-Nisei regiment was being created and called for volunteers. At that point, the VVV disbanded and the young men joined the 442nd Regimental Combat Team.

22 Kathryn Shankle, "Patriots Under Fire: Japanese Americans in World War II.' U.S. Department of Defense, Center of Military History. Internet Citation, June 6, 2014.

23 Ibid.

24 Franklin Odo. *No Sword to Bury: Japanese-Americans in Hawai'i During World War II.* (Philadelphia: Temple University Press, 2004), 167-180.

25 Tabrah, 49.

26 Tabrah, 50.

27 Ibid. 52.

28 Ibid. 58.

Chapter Eight – Bodh Gaya
1 Alan Trevithick, *A Jerusalem of the Buddhists in British India (1874-1949).* (Cambridge: Harvard University, 1988), 1.

The Gayawals claimed that they were created by Brahma, and the Shaivites were established as a Hindu monastic order by the Advaita philosopher Sankara in the ninth century and worshiped the God Shiva. They came to the Mahabodhi Temple and laid claim somewhere between 1590 and 1690.

2 Ibid., 3.

3 Karl Klostermaier's "Hindu Views of Buddhism," *Canadian Contributions to Buddhist Studies.* (Waterloo: Wilfred Laurie University Press, 1979), 64.

⁴ Ibid. 65.

⁵ Tara Nancy Doyle. *Bodh Gaya: Journeys to the Diamond Throne and the Feet of* Gayasur. (Cambridge: Harvard University, 1997), 161.

⁶ Ibid. 161.

⁷ *Diaries*, Colombo: National Archives of Sri Lanka, Vol. 6, 57.

⁸ Trevithick, 25.

⁹ *Diaries*, 62.

¹⁰ Ibid.,1/28/1891.

¹¹ Trevithick, 26.

¹² Dharmapala's Diaries, 3/9/1891.

¹³ Ibid.

¹⁴ William Lansdowne, Collection of Correspondence in India (LCCI), vol. 21, 8/26/1891) 34-36.

¹⁵ Diaries – 10/30/1891, 245.

¹⁶ LCCI, vol. 21, 11/6/1891, 78-89.

¹⁷ *Maha Bodhi Journal* vol. 16, August 1908, 75-80.

Chapter Nine – Kahana
¹ **"Beautiful Kahana"** - Words & music by Mary J. Montano

(Written about Mary Foster and her home at Kahana Bay)

Source: King's Hawaiian Melodies - Written for Mary E. Foster and her beautiful country home, Kalahikiola, on the windward side of O`ahu at Kahana. Translated by Mary Pukui Copyright 1915, 1942, 1963 by Charles E. King. What is fascinating in the song is the reference to Mary being "the loving heart of India." Her deep spiritual connection to India was so much a part of her life and character that it is celebrated in a popular local song.

2 Clarice B. Taylor, *Tales About Hawaii: The Robinson Family*. (Honolulu: Honolulu Star Bulletin, 1952), 30.

3 Robert Stauffer, 2.

4 Ibid. 4.

5 Ibid.

6 Ibid.

7 The way the land division traditionally worked was:

Each mokupuni was divided into several moku, the largest units within each island, usually wedge-shaped and running from the mountain crest to shore. Oʻahu was divided into six moku. Each moku was divided into ahupuaʻa, also narrow wedge-shaped land sections that ran from the mountains to the sea. The size of the ahupuaʻa depended on the resources of the area with poorer agricultural regions split into larger ahupuaʻa to compensate for the relative lack of natural abundance. Each ahupuaʻa was ruled by an aliʻi or local chief and administered by a konohiki, or caretaker.

Within the ahupuaʻa, ʻili were smaller divisions (two or three per ahupuaʻa) that constituted the estate of the chief. Each ʻili could be formed of noncontiguous pieces called lele, or jumps. Moʻo were sections of the ʻili that were arable; usually these agricultural units did not extend to the sea. Smaller yet were the kuleana, or land tracts used by the common people for cultivation of crops. The size of kuleana, like the size of ahupuaʻa, depended on the natural fertility and abundance of the land.

8 Stauffer, 11-13.

9 In 1856, Annie Keohokalole and her husband Kapaʻakea put all of their holdings into a trust for the benefit of her son, David Kalākaua, and then sold it in 1857 to AhSing also known as Apakana, a Chinese merchant – Legislative Reference Bureau Report, 2.

10 Much of King Kamehameha III's land was so heavily mortgaged that the

Haole-dominated government at some point took the land, paid off the mortgages, and set aside an allowance for the king.

[11] Stauffer, 2.

[12] Stauffer, 168.

[13] Ibid., 170.

[14] Hawaii Legislative Research Bureau Report: *Kahana Valley,* 4; Conveyance 111:13.

[15] Ibid, 4.

[16] Ibid.

[17] "State's Offer for Kahana," *Honolulu Star Bulletin*, July 9, 1965.

[18] Ibid.

[19] Legislative Research Bureau Report, 7.

[20] Ibid, 20.

Chapter Ten – Colombo
[1] Conversation with Mala Weerasekera, Colombo, Sri Lanka, May 15, 1999.

[2] The 1915 Riots in Colombo are an important part of Sri Lankan history.

[3] Ananda Guruge, 727.

[4] Ibid.

[5] Kumari Jayawardene, *The White Woman's Other Burden: Western Women and South Asia During British Rule.* (New York: Routledge Books, 1995), 8.

[6] Ibid. 164.

[7] Ibid. 166.

Chapter 11 – Honolulu

1   *Mary Foster.* File at Pacific Collection, Hamilton Library, University of Hawai'i, 1965.

2   Regarding the photograph, it is difficult to determine if it is a composite painted backdrop or an actual scene off the balcony of a building in South Asia. If it is the latter, then it may be evidence that Mary Foster traveled to India. If we look at the photo as an actual on-site portrait, certain elements beyond the balustrade behind Mary's image could be seen as Asian. Could this be Bodh Gaya? In the photo, as well, there is a large stone sculpture of a *naga*, possibly Mucchalinda, the King of Snakes, who shaded the Buddha during his awakening process. It is not possible to determine where Mary is sitting. Perhaps on the roof of a structure across the road from the temple. It could be Bodh Gaya. She could have traveled there. Imperfect as it is, the snapshot of her portrait in the hospital in Sri Lanka may be the sole bit of evidence that she traveled to South Asia and sites sacred to Buddhism.

REFERENCES

Agarwal, C.V. *The Buddhist and Theosophical Movements: 1873 – 2001.*
Calcutta: Maha Bodhi Society of India, 2001.

Aitken, Molly Emma. *Meeting the Buddha: On Pilgrimage in Buddhist India.*
New York: Riverhead Books, 1995.

Arnold, Edwin. *The Light of Asia or The Great Renunciation.* London: Kegan
Paul, Trench, Trubner & Co., 1892.

Bancroft, Anne. *The Buddha Speaks.* Boston: Shambala Press, 2000.

Bartholomeusz, Tessa. *Women Under The Bo Tree.* Cambridge: Cambridge
University Press, 1994.

Besant, Annie. *Buddhism.* Madras: The Theosophical Publishing House, 1899.

---. *Man and His Bodies.* Madras: The Theosophical Society, 1896

Blavatsky, Helena Petrova. *Isis Unveiled.* Pasadena: Theosophical University
Press, 1889.

---. *The Key to Theosophy.* Pasadena: Theosophical University Press, 1889.

Bouslag, Charles. S. "Doctor Auguste Jean Baptiste and Evelyn Oliver
Marques." *The Hawaiian Journal of History,* vol. 26 (1992).

Buddhaghosa, Bhadantacariya. *The Path of Purification (Visuddhimagga).*
Onalaska: BPS Pariyatti Publishing, 1975.

Coffman, Tom. *Nation Within: The Story of America's Annexation of the Nation
of Hawaiʻi.* Kanʻeohe: Epicenter, 1997.

Daws, Gavin. *Honolulu: the First Century. The Story of the town to 1876.*
Honolulu: University of Hawai ʻI Press, 2006.

de Waal, Edmund. *The Hare with Amber Eyes.* New York: Farrar, Straus and
Giroux, 2010.

Doughtery, Michael. *To Steal A Kingdom.* Waimanalo: Island Press, 1992.

Doyle, Tara Nancy. *Bodh Gaya: Journeys to the Diamond Throne and the Feet of Gayasur.* Ph.D. Dissertation, Harvard University, June 1997.

Fields, Rick. *How the Swans Came to the Lake: A Narrative History of Buddhism in America.* Boulder: Shambala Publications, 1981.

Fornander, Abraham. *An Account of the Polynesian People: Its Origins and Migrations, and the Ancient History of the Hawaiian People to the times of Kamehameha I.* London: Trubner and Co., 1878.

Geschwender, James A. "The Interplay Between Class and National Consciousness in Hawai'i, 1850-1950." Paper for the National Institutes of Mental Health, no date.

Gombrich, Richard, and Gananath Obeysekera. *Buddhism Transformed: Religious Change in Sri Lanka.* Princeton: Princeton University Press, 1988.

Guruge, Ananda. *Anagarika Dharmapala.* Colombo: The National Department of Cultural Affairs, 1967.

---. *Anagarika Dharmapala: Return to Righteousness.* Colombo: The Ministry of Education and Cultural Affairs, Government Publications, 1965.

Hackler, Rhoda. "Foster Botanical Garden 1853-1990: Contributions of a Doctor, a Donor, a Forester, and a Park Achitect," *The Hawaiian Historical Society,* vol. 43, 2009.

Hecker, Hellmuth. *Buddhist Women at the Time of the Buddha.* Kandy: Buddhist Publication Society, 1982.

Houghton, Walter R. *The Parliament of Religions and Religious Congresses at the World's Columbian Exposition.* Chicago: F. Tennyson Neely Publisher, 1894.

Hunter, Louise H. *Buddhism in Hawai'i: Its Impact on a Yankee Community.* Honolulu: University of Hawai'i Press, 1971.

Hustace, Frank Ward. III. *Victoria Ward and Her Family.* Honolulu: Victoria Ward, 2000.

Kirch, Patrick Vinton. *A Shark Going Inland is My Chief.* Berkeley: University of California, 2012.

Jayawardena, Kumari. *The White Woman's Other Burden: Western Women and South Asia During British Rule.* London; Routledge, 1995.

Kamakau, Samuel M. *Ruling Chiefs of Hawaiʻi.* Honolulu: Kamehameha Schools, copyrighted 1961.

Karpiel, Frank J. "A Multinational Fraternity: Freemasonry in Hawaiʻi, 1843-1905." *The Hawaiian Journal of History,* vol. 34 (2000).

---. "Theosophy, Culture, and Politics in Honolulu, 1890-1920." *The Hawaiian Journal of History,* vol. 30 (1996).

Karunaratne, Saddamangala. *Olcott's Contribution to the Buddhist Renaissance.* Colombo: Ministry of Cultural Affairs, 1967.

Kashima, Tetsuden. *Buddhism in America: The Social Organization of an Ethnic Religious Institution.* London: Greenwood Press, 1977.

Kuykendall, Ralph S. *The Hawaiian Kingdom: Volume III (1874-1893) The Kalakaua Dynasty.* Honolulu: University of Hawaii Press, 1967.

Lansdowne, William, *Lansdowne Collection of Correspondence in India (LCCI).* (London: Government Papers, Vol. 21, 8/26/1891), 34.

Liliʻuokalani. *Hawaiʻi's Story by Hawaiʻi's Queen.* Rutland, Vermont: Charles E. Tuttle Company, 1898, 1964.

Linnekin, Jocelyn. *Sacred Queens and Women of Consequence.* Ann Arbor: The University of Michigan Press, 1990.

Lipton, Thomas J. *Lipton's Autobiography.* Boston: Duffield Green, 1932.

Murcott, Susan. *First Buddhist Women: Poems and Stories of Awakening.* Berkeley: Parallax Press, 2006.

Musaeus-Higgins, Marie. *Stories from the History of Ceylon.* Kandy: Lakehouse Publishers, 1999.

Olcott, Henry Steele. *Old Diary Leaves (1878-1883)*. Chennai: The Theosophical Publishing House, 2006.

---. *The Buddhist Catechism*. Madras: The Theosophical Publishing House, 1881.

Prasoon, Shrikant. *Anagarika Dharmapala: In Spiritual Quadruplets*. Varanasi: Pilgrims Publishing, 2007.

Prothero, Stephen. *The White Buddhist: The Asian Odyssey of Henry Steele Olcott*. Delhi: Sri Sat Guru Publications, 1996.

Pukui, Mary Kawena and Samuel H. Ebert. *Hawaiian Dictionary*. Honolulu: University of Hawai'i Press, 1986. 6th Edition.

Ratnatunga, Sinha. *They Turned the Tide: The 100 Year History of the Mahabodhi Society of Sri*

Lanka. Colombo: Sri Lankan Government Publications, 1992.

Sangharakshita, Bhiksu. *Flames in Darkness: The Life and Sayings of Anagarika Dharmapala*. Pune: Triratna Granthamala Publishers, 1980, 1995.

---. *Anagarika Dharmapala: A Biographical Sketch*. Kandy: Buddhist Publication Society, 1983.

Seager, Richard Hughes. *The World's Parliament of Religions: The East/West Encounter, Chicago, 1893*. Bloomington and Indianapolis: Indiana University Press, 1995.

Seewalee Thero. *Anagarika Dharmapala and the Buddhagaya Centre*. Gaya: Mahabodhi Society of India, 2007.

Seiden, Allan. Unpublished manuscript (partial) of the Robinson Family, 2016.

Sen, Chandra. *A Short Life Sketch of Sri Mat Anagarika Dharmapala*. Panadura: Mahabodhi Society, 1997.

H. L. Seneviratne. *The Work of Kings: The New Buddhism in Sri Lanka*. Chicago: University of Chicago Press, 2000.

Silva, Noenoe K. *Aloha Betrayed: Native Hawaiian Resistance to American Colonialism.*Durham & London: Duke University Press, 2004.

Snelling, John. *The Buddhist Handbook: A Complete Guide to Buddhist Schools, Teachings, Practice, and History.* New York: Barnes and Noble Books, 1998.

Stauffer, Robert, Jr. *Kahana: How the Land Was Lost.* Honolulu: University of Hawai'i Press, 2004.

Tabrah, Ruth. *A Grateful Past, A Promising Future: The First 100 Years of Honpa Hongwanji in Hawai'i.* Honpa Hongwanji Centennial Committee, 1989.

Tambiah, Stanley Jeyaraja. *Buddhism Betrayed? Religion, Politics, and Violence in Sri Lanka.* Chicago: The University of Chicago Press, 1992.

Taylor, Clarice. *The James Robinson Family. Tales About Hawaii.* Honolulu: Honolulu Star Bulletin, 1952, 1967.

The Mahabodhi Society of India. *The Mahabodhi Centenary (1891-1991).* Calcutta: the Mahabodhi Publishers, 1991.

Trevithick, Alan. *The Mahabodhi Society in Bodh Gaya*, unpublished Ph.D. Dissertation, 1987.

Woolf, Leonard. *The Village in the Jungle.* Oxford: Oxford University Press, 1913.

Yardley, Maili and Miriam Rodgers. *The History of Kapiolani Hospital.* Honolulu: Ku Pa'a Incorporated, 1941.

APPENDIX

1. *Beautiful Kahana*

Beautiful Kahana

Words & music by Mary J. Montano

Mau loa nō ko`u mahalo nui	I admire everlastingly
I ka nani pūnono o Kahana	The glowing beauty of Kahana
Ka moani `a`ala anuhea	The sweet wind-borne perfume
O nā pali a`o Ko`olauloa	Of the cliffs of Ko`olauloa
Hui:	Chorus:
`O ka home ia o ka wahine	This is the home of the lady
Pu`uwai aloha a `Īnia	Of the loving heart of India
He pua ua mili ani `ia	A flower lovingly fondled
E ka Mālualua ki`i wai	By the Mālualua ki`i wai breeze
`O Kalāhikiola nō ka `oi	Kalāhikiola is the greatest
He pu`ulena ia na ka maka	It holds one's admiration
Kohu kīhene pua ka u`i	As pretty as a basket of flowers
I luluhe i ka `ae o ke kai	Leaning over at the edge of the sea
Hui:	Chorus:
He maile kaluhea ia la`i	Like the large leaved maile in the calm
Ha`aheo a ke ao nāulu	Proud in the presence of the rain clouds
Ulu a`e ka mana`o he aloha	It inspires an expression of love
Ia kuini pua `o Kahana	For the flower queen of Kahana

Source: King's Hawaiian Melodies - Written for Mary E. Foster and her beautiful country home, Kalahikiola, on the windward side of O'ahu at Kahana. Verse 1, stanza 2, "the loving heart of India" refers to Mary Foster's Bahai faith and her monetary gifts to build a Bahai temple in India. Many of her charitable acts in Hawai`i were done quietly and unknown to the general public, but the lasting gift was her Honolulu home, now part of the famous Foster Botanical Gardens.

Foster Gardens is a 20-acre oasis in downtown Honolulu. Mary (part-Hawaiian) and her ship owner husband Thomas purchased the property from Dr. William Hillebrand, a German botanist, in 1880. Mrs. Foster purchased additional acreage and Princess Lili'uokalani added to the gardens by purchasing the adjoining property from the estate of Queen Kalama, wife of Kamehameha III. Before her death, Lili'uokalani, who kept a cottage on the grounds, transferred title to the Civic Federation of Honolulu, to be used as a park. Mrs. Foster also bequeathed her garden to the city of Honolulu in 1930. Both properties were combined and became the Foster Botanical Gardens. Translated by Mary Pukui. Copyright 1915, 1942, 1963 by Charles E. King